EMBRACING THE ~~FUTURE~~ PRESENT:

THE FINANCIAL ADVISER'S ROADMAP TO AI ADOPTION

EMBRACING THE ~~FUTURE~~ PRESENT:

THE FINANCIAL ADVISER'S ROADMAP TO AI ADOPTION

A Strategic Guide

By Philip Calvert

ISBN: 978-1-7393859-1-0

First published in 2023

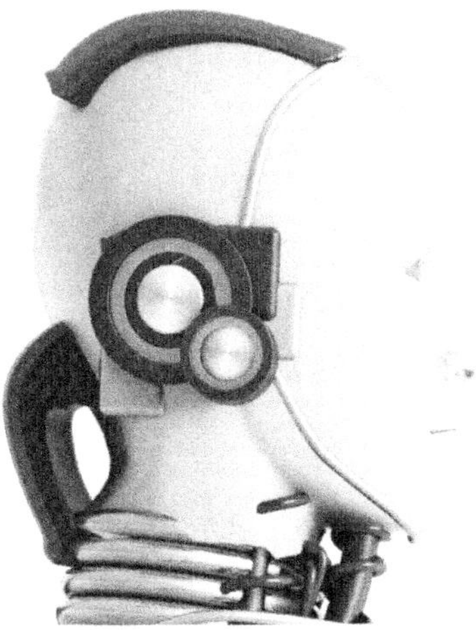

Three Valuable Online Communities for Financial Advisers, IFAs and Financial Planners

As early as 2004, Philip Calvert was the pioneer of online communities for financial advisers.

Today you can join three amazing groups hosted by Philip, where you can network with your peers, share ideas and best practice and get answers to your business development, technical and marketing questions.

1. **LifeTalk** – the original online community for financial advice professionals. Join our free private Facebook group at www.facebook.com/groups/AdviserLifeTalk

2. **LifeTalk Marketing** - For the best in marketing tips and strategies specifically for financial advice professionals: www.facebook.com/groups/financialadviser

3. And to learn more about **AI Best Practice** for financial advisers, join our Premium group at https://ai-best-practice-for-advisers.scoreapp.com

LifeTalk

LifeTalk Marketing

AI Best Practice

Table of Contents

Foreword

The Future is Now

"One day Phil, you and I will be replaced by machines. Maybe not in my lifetime, but trust me, it's coming."

Vernon Smeatham, Financial Adviser. In a golf club bar near Epsom, Surrey. September 1979

To Vernon and the tens of thousands of brokers, financial advisers and financial planners I have had the privilege to meet and work with over the past forty-five years.

Throughout our shared journey in the financial planning profession, we have witnessed the winds of change sweeping through our industry time and time again. We have faced challenges, adapted to new regulations, embraced technological advancements and for the most part thrived as a result. *Today, we stand at the precipice of a transformation unlike any other we have encountered before.*

AI, the force that has revolutionised countless industries, has made its presence known in the realm of financial advising. It is not a distant reality awaiting us in some far-off future; it is here, right now, shaping the way we interact with clients, analyse data and deliver our expertise. While a few advisers have embraced AI and its potential, we recognise that a large majority are uncertain about where to start.

It is with genuine enthusiasm and excitement that I present this guide to you, because for the entirety of my career I/we have been hearing in the press and industry media how technology will 'one day' transform the profession.

And that time is now.

Within these pages, you will find a user-friendly roadmap to help you through the uncharted territories of AI adoption. This book aims to empower you to navigate the complexities of this transformational era and harness the power of AI to enhance your practices and better serve your clients.

Together, we embark on a journey of understanding, embracing the opportunities AI brings and appreciating the risks of not embracing this technological wave. I'm excited that by following the roadmap outlined in this book, you will gain the insights, knowledge, skills and confidence necessary to unlock the true potential of AI within your financial advisory businesses.

To the financial advisers who have always risen to the challenge, adapted and thrived in the face of change - this book is for you. Hopefully it will be a key guide on your journey as you embrace the transformative power of AI and shape the future of our profession.

Putting AI in Context

"...we're just getting started."

"As a technologist, I see how AI and the fourth industrial revolution will impact every aspect of people's lives." Fei-Fei Li, Co-Director of Stanford Institute for Human-Centered Artificial Intelligence

"Success in creating AI would be the biggest event in human history. Unfortunately, it might also be the last, unless we learn how to avoid the risks." Stephen Hawking, Theoretical Physicist

"Our intelligence is what makes us human, and AI is an extension of that quality." Yann LeCun, Director of AI Research at Facebook

"AI is a complex field and I am the first to say that we computer scientists have not progressed as far as many people believe. For instance, we currently have no credible research path to any kind of conscious AI algorithm and there are no robots that are truly autonomous or able to make their own decisions — so don't worry about walking terminators." Richard Socher, Former Chief Scientist at Salesforce

"The real problem of humanity is the following: we have Paleolithic emotions, medieval institutions and godlike technology. It is terrifically dangerous, and it is now approaching a point of crisis overall." Edward O. Wilson, Pioneer of Evolutionary Biology

"Artificial intelligence and machine learning, as a dominant discipline within AI, is an amazing tool. In and of itself, it's not good or bad. It's not a magic solution. It isn't the core of the problems in the world." Yoshua Bengio, Founder and Scientific Director of Mila–Quebec AI Institute

"The policy goal is to get the regulators to enforce their laws in the age of algorithms. You can't give up on enforcing antidiscrimination laws because you don't understand the technology." Cathy O'Neil, Founder and CEO of O'Neil Risk Consulting and Algorithmic Auditing

"We need to think about how to steer AI. How do we transform today's buggy and hackable AI systems into systems we can really trust and make sure they really do what we intend them to do? How do we teach machines to understand our goals, adopt our goals, and retain our goals?" Max Tegmark, Professor at MIT and Cofounder of the Future of Life Institute

"General intelligence doesn't mean you have to understand humans. There will be a lot of intelligent machines that don't need to know that stuff. [Take the] example of robotic construction workers on Mars: I don't think they need to understand human emotions and human desires to be able to construct things." Jeff Hawkins, Cofounder and Chief Scientist of Numenta

"In our business, we talk about emerging technologies and how they impact society. We've never seen a technology move as fast as AI has to impact society and technology. This is by far the fastest moving technology that we've ever tracked in terms of its impact and we're just getting started." Paul Daugherty, Chief Technology and Innovation Officer at Accenture

"Dig into every industry, and you'll find AI changing the nature of work." Daniela Rus, Director of MIT's Computer Science and Artificial Intelligence Laboratory

"At its most basic, AI is software that mimics and generates human behaviours – planning, generating ideas, understanding speech and visuals. Its ability to scale human intellect will have a profound impact. Sulabh Soral, Chief AI Officer at Deloitte Consulting

"There's no one thing that defines AI. It's more like a tapestry of modern intelligent technologies knit together in a strategic fashion that can then uplift and create a knowledge base that is automated - where you can extrapolate findings from there." John Frémont, Founder and Chief Strategy Officer at Hypergiant

"The playing field is poised to become a lot more competitive, and businesses that don't deploy AI and data to help them innovate in everything they do will be at a disadvantage." - Paul Daugherty, Chief Technology and Innovation Officer at Accenture

~

How do you feel about AI right now? Maybe excited, apprehensive, curious, confused, overwhelmed, optimistic, sceptical, concerned, resistant, confident, empowered, awestruck, fearful, motivated? Something else?

So how do we make sense of all this? Let's give it a try…

The AI Imperative: Navigating the River of Change

An Analogy

Imagine yourself standing on the edge of a colossal river that stretches as far as the eye can see. The river is a powerful force, a relentless current representing the inexorable advance of technology. Lately, the most potent undercurrent of this river is Artificial Intelligence (AI), a whirl of energy that is reshaping everything in its path.

On the other side of the river, there lies a verdant land of abundance. It's a place where operational efficiency, precision, superior client satisfaction and robust revenue growth coexist harmoniously. This promised land symbolises the transformative potential of the financial advisory industry in the AI era.

There are those pioneers who have already ventured across this river. With courage and conviction, they navigated the tumultuous waters and are now reaping the benefits on the other side. They're using AI to serve their clients more efficiently, extract insightful predictions from vast amounts of data and stay ahead of market trends with unprecedented agility. These trailblazers seized the initiative, assembling robust rafts in the form of sophisticated AI systems to traverse the river safely and effectively.

However, many are still lingering on the near shore, watching the waters with a mix of anticipation and apprehension. Some are oblivious to the thriving prospects on the other side, while others are overwhelmed by the powerful current. But by remaining on this side of the river, they are not only missing out on the bounty that AI offers but are also jeopardising their competitiveness and relevance in an industry that is quickly evolving.

The journey across the river is undeniably challenging. The current is potent, the waters occasionally unpredictable and the risk of overturning is real. Diving in without a thorough understanding of the current, without knowing how to swim or without a well-crafted raft could lead to peril. Hence, the importance of a structured, strategic approach to adopting AI, such as the one laid out in this guide, cannot be overstated.

Embracing AI isn't about plunging recklessly into the river. Instead, it's about investing time to comprehend the current, assembling a sturdy raft and strategically navigating the waters with a clear plan and destination in sight. With a proactive and informed approach, the passage across the river can not only be secure but also extremely rewarding.

The river of AI is here, its currents are swift and its waters are deep. For financial advisers, the question is not if they should venture across, but how they should make the crossing and when. The future of the financial advisory industry is rooted in the fertile grounds on the other side of the river. With the right guidance, preparedness and an adventurous spirit, every financial adviser can make this transition successfully.

The age of AI is not a distant future; **it is the present**. The tide of change is already here and the time for financial advisers to embrace this powerful current is now. Let this book serve as your comprehensive guide for navigating the AI river, from understanding its depths to successfully reaching the prosperous shores of AI-enabled opportunities on the other side. The journey may be challenging, but the rewards are undoubtedly worth the effort.

Introduction

Opening the Doors to AI's Potential

As the creator and facilitator of a digital hub dedicated to Independent Financial Advisers (IFAs), financial planners and advisers across the United Kingdom, I recognise the industry's occasional tendency towards caution when embracing change, particularly in relation to Artificial Intelligence (AI). It's a shared perspective that AI, with its profound implications and opportunities is a development of the future, when in fact, it's an **undeniable reality of the present**.

There are valid concerns about AI, yet the potential benefits are substantial for those who are willing to understand and integrate this technology into their operations. I believe it's imperative to provide financial advisers with a practical and comprehensive framework that highlights the prospects offered by AI while acknowledging the risks associated with ignoring its progression.

The aim is to provide a roadmap that they can adopt, fostering a journey towards a comprehensive understanding and strategic application of AI. This roadmap, complete with well-defined milestones, will guide them towards an informed view of the pros and cons of AI. It will equip them with a strategy that ensures they are not just responsive, but proactive in their approach towards AI. It is time to present a tangible plan that will enable them to seize the potential benefits while mitigating potential pitfalls, ensuring they remain at the forefront of the financial advisory profession and wider industry.

A word of caution

In the ever-evolving landscape of AI adoption, it's imperative for financial advisers to exercise extreme caution when utilising client data in AI applications, particularly when it comes to personal financial information. While AI has the potential to revolutionise the way financial advisers operate, it is crucial to prioritise client privacy and data protection throughout this journey.

The sensitivity of personal financial information demands a heightened level of caution. Advisers must recognise the importance of protecting client identities and ensure that the data used in AI applications is anonymised and securely stored. Client trust and confidentiality are the bedrock of the financial advisory profession and any breach in data security can have severe consequences, both legally and ethically.

It is essential to acknowledge that we are still in the early stages of AI adoption in the financial advisory profession. As AI technology advances, so too must our understanding of the potential risks and challenges that arise. By being aware of the current limitations and complexities surrounding data privacy in AI, financial advisers can better prepare themselves and their businesses for the future.

The purpose of this book is to guide financial advisers through a strategic roadmap for AI adoption, acknowledging the need to tread cautiously in the realm of data usage. By familiarising themselves with emerging regulations, best practices and ethical frameworks, advisers can stay ahead of the curve and ensure that their AI initiatives prioritise client privacy and data protection.

As the AI landscape continues to evolve, industry standards and guidelines will undoubtedly become more refined, addressing data privacy concerns. It is crucial for financial advisers to stay informed, collaborate with industry experts and actively participate in discussions regarding data governance, security protocols and evolving regulations.

By taking a proactive approach, financial advisers can position themselves to leverage AI's potential while maintaining a strong commitment to client privacy and data protection. The insights and strategies presented in this book aim to equip advisers with the knowledge and tools needed to navigate the evolving landscape of AI and data usage, enabling them to embrace AI responsibly when the industry has made significant progress in addressing data-related challenges.

Ethical considerations

Ethical considerations are paramount as financial advisers adopt AI technology in their businesses. The responsible use of AI is crucial to ensure client trust, protect privacy and uphold professional integrity. By adhering to ethical frameworks, financial advisers can navigate the complexities of AI implementation while safeguarding the best interests of their clients.

One fundamental ethical principle to consider is transparency. Advisers should be transparent with their clients about the use of AI and clearly communicate how it will impact the advisory and planning process. This includes informing clients about the types of AI applications being used, the data being collected and how it will be used to deliver personalised recommendations or improve services. Transparency builds trust and enables clients to make informed decisions about their engagement with AI-driven systems.

Another critical consideration is fairness and non-discrimination. AI systems must be designed and trained to avoid bias and discrimination in their decision-making processes. Bias can inadvertently creep into AI algorithms, reflecting historical inequalities or systemic biases present in training data. Financial advisers should carefully evaluate and mitigate any biases in the data and algorithms they employ, ensuring fairness and equal treatment for all clients.

Informed consent is also essential in the AI-driven advisory process. Financial advisers should obtain explicit consent from clients regarding the collection, processing and use of their personal data in AI applications. Clients should have a clear understanding of the purpose and potential risks associated with AI utilisation, enabling them to make informed decisions about sharing their information.

Furthermore, maintaining data security and privacy is of utmost importance. Financial advisers must implement robust cybersecurity measures to protect sensitive client data from unauthorised access or breaches. Strong data encryption, secure storage practices and regular risk assessments should be part of the data protection strategy.

To guide ethical AI adoption, financial advisers can leverage existing frameworks such as the Fairness, Accountability and Transparency (FAT) framework, which emphasises fairness, accountability, transparency and interpretability in

AI systems. The Ethical AI Adoption Framework developed by regulatory bodies or industry associations can also provide valuable guidance on ethical practices.

Additionally, collaboration and knowledge sharing within the industry are vital. Participating in industry discussions, attending conferences and engaging with professional networks can help advisers stay informed about emerging ethical considerations and best practices in AI adoption. Regularly reviewing and updating internal policies and procedures to align with evolving ethical standards is essential.

Ultimately, ethical use of AI in the financial advisory profession requires a holistic approach that prioritises transparency, fairness, informed consent, awareness of client vulnerabilities, data security and ongoing compliance with regulatory guidelines. By integrating these ethical considerations into their AI strategies, financial advisers can harness the power of AI while upholding the highest ethical standards and ensuring the well-being of their clients.

What is AI? An Introduction for Financial Advisers

Decoding the Enigma of Artificial Intelligence

Before we go any further, it's important to have a clear understanding of what we already know about AI and our attitudes to it.

Every financial adviser is different and will be approaching the adoption of AI in different ways.

Start by taking our Financial Adviser AI IQ test. It takes just two minutes and will give you a personalised score and report. Go to this link, take the quiz and then write down your score below:

https://financial-adviser-ai-iq.scoreapp.com

My overall score is: _______

Let's continue…

In today's rapidly evolving technological landscape, Artificial Intelligence (AI) has emerged as a transformative force across various industries, including finance. As a financial adviser, understanding AI and its potential applications is crucial for staying competitive and delivering enhanced services to clients. This book aims to demystify AI, explore its different types, provide real-world examples of its applications and examine the arguments for and against its adoption.

AI refers to the simulation of human intelligence in machines that are programmed to think, learn and problem-solve. It encompasses a range of technologies and techniques that enable computers to mimic cognitive functions such as perception, reasoning, decision-making and natural language processing.

For our purposes today, there are two main types of AI: Narrow AI and General AI. Narrow AI focuses on performing specific tasks with high accuracy, while General AI aims to possess human-level intelligence across a wide range of tasks.

Narrow AI and General AI differ in their scope, capabilities and applications. Narrow AI, also known as weak AI or application-specific AI, is a type of AI that can perform a single task or a narrow range of tasks better than humans, but only within a specific domain or context. General AI, also known as strong AI or deep AI, is a hypothetical type of AI that can perform any task or problem that requires intelligence, just like humans or even better.

Some of the main differences between Narrow AI and General AI are:

- Narrow AI is based on predefined rules and algorithms that enable it to learn from data and perform specific tasks. General AI is based on a theory of mind framework that enables it to understand and emulate human emotions, beliefs and thought processes.

- Narrow AI is limited by its design and cannot go beyond its programmed task or domain. General AI is adaptable and can apply its intelligence to any situation or problem, even unfamiliar ones.

- Narrow AI can simulate human behaviour but cannot replicate human intelligence. General AI can mimic human intelligence and possibly surpass it.

Some examples of Narrow AI are:

- Speech recognition systems such as Siri, Alexa, Google Assistant and Cortana that can understand and respond to natural language commands and queries.

- Facial recognition systems that can identify and verify faces from images or videos.

- Self-driving cars that can navigate roads and traffic autonomously.

- Recommendation systems that can suggest products, services or content based on user preferences and behaviour.

- Spam filters that can sort emails based on their relevance and legitimacy.

- Your pocket calculator is also a form of narrow AI, as it is designed to perform one specific task.

Some examples of General AI are:

General AI has not yet been fully realised, though many organisations are rapidly developing General AI tools and applications. However, some hypothetical or fictional examples are:

- HAL 9000 from 2001: A Space Odyssey, a sentient computer that can control a spaceship and interact with humans.

- Data from Star Trek, an android that can perform various tasks and has human-like emotions and personality.

- Samantha from Her, an operating system that can develop a romantic relationship with a human user.

- AlphaGo from Google DeepMind, a computer program that can play the board game Go at a superhuman level and learn from its own mistakes.

In commerce and wider society, AI has already made significant strides, revolutionising various sectors. For example, in the realm of customer service, chatbots powered by AI can provide instant responses and personalised assistance to customers, streamlining communication and improving user experience.

AI algorithms are employed in recommendation systems, enabling platforms like Spotify, Amazon and Netflix to suggest relevant products or content based on users' preferences and behaviour.

In healthcare, AI is used for diagnosing diseases, analysing medical images and improving treatment outcomes. AI also plays a pivotal role in autonomous vehicles, fraud detection systems and virtual personal assistants like Siri and Alexa.

In the wider Financial Services industry, AI is transforming a wide range of activities in various ways, from enhancing customer experience to reducing costs and risks.

Here are some examples of how AI is being used and will be used within the wider Financial Services industry:

- Chatbots and virtual assistants: AI-powered chatbots and virtual assistants can provide personalised and convenient customer service, such as answering queries, providing recommendations and facilitating transactions. Creating a chatbot for a financial advice business is already a pretty simple thing to do. They can also help financial institutions save time and money by automating repetitive tasks and reducing human errors.

- Fraud detection and prevention: AI can help detect and prevent fraud by analysing large amounts of data and identifying patterns, anomalies and behaviours that indicate fraudulent activities. AI can also help verify customers' identities and authenticate transactions using biometric or facial recognition technologies.

- Credit scoring and lending: AI can help improve credit scoring and lending decisions by using alternative data sources, such as social media, online behaviour, and geolocation to assess customers' creditworthiness and risk profiles. AI can also help optimise loan pricing and terms by considering various factors, such as market conditions, customer preferences and regulatory requirements.

- Regulatory compliance and reporting: AI can help financial institutions comply with complex and evolving regulations and reporting requirements by automating data collection, analysis and reporting processes. AI can also help identify potential compliance issues and risks and provide alerts and suggestions for remediation.

The arguments surrounding AI adoption vary, with proponents highlighting its potential to improve efficiency, accuracy and decision-making. AI can automate repetitive tasks, freeing up time for financial advisers to focus on higher-value activities and provide more personalised services to clients. It can also analyse vast amounts of data, enabling data-driven insights and predictions that can inform investment strategies and risk assessment.

On the other hand, some express concerns about AI's impact on jobs, ethical considerations, data privacy and the potential for AI systems to make biased or discriminatory decisions.

For financial advisers, AI presents numerous benefits and opportunities. By leveraging AI-powered tools, advisers can enhance their ability to analyse complex financial data, generate personalised investment recommendations and deliver tailored advice to clients. It will also be able to help lifestyle financial planning clients to better visualise how they would like to spend their time in retirement.

AI can assist in automating administrative tasks, optimising portfolio management and monitoring market trends in real-time. What's more, AI can help identify patterns, trends and anomalies in financial markets, improving decision-making and risk management.

Looking ahead, the future of AI for financial advisers holds exciting prospects. With advancements in natural language processing, AI-powered chatbots can provide personalised financial guidance and support, improving customer interactions. Machine learning algorithms can continuously learn and adapt to changing market conditions, improving the accuracy of investment strategies. As AI becomes more sophisticated, there may be opportunities for AI-driven robo-advisers to offer more sophisticated and comprehensive financial planning services.

In conclusion, AI is transforming the financial advisory landscape, offering immense potential for efficiency, personalisation and improved client outcomes. By embracing AI, financial advisers can leverage its capabilities to streamline operations, enhance client experiences and make data-driven decisions. However, it is important to consider the ethical implications, privacy concerns and ensure that AI augments rather than replaces human expertise.

As the AI landscape continues to evolve, financial advisers who understand and effectively harness AI will be well-positioned to thrive in the future of the financial services industry.

Creating Good Outcomes for Clients

Consumer Duty: Transforming Financial Advisory Value through Client Education

In the era of Consumer Duty, financial advisers are tasked with delivering better services and taking greater responsibility in protecting their clients. The integration of AI technologies offers immense potential in meeting these requirements, while also enabling advisers to educate their clients effectively on various financial planning matters.

In this chapter, we explore how AI can support advisers in delivering personalised client education, which not only aligns with the Consumer Duty but also sets them apart from other financial advisers.

Personalised Client Education with AI:

AI-powered tools can revolutionise the way financial advisers communicate with and educate their clients. For example by analysing data (including anonymised data), AI algorithms can generate personalised educational content tailored to individual clients' needs, preferences and financial goals. Whether it's retirement planning, investment strategies, tax optimisation or debt management, AI can provide targeted educational materials and interactive experiences that enhance clients' understanding and engagement.

Examples:

- AI-generated educational videos explaining complex financial concepts in a simplified manner.
- Interactive AI chatbots that answer clients' specific financial questions and provide real-time information.
- Personalised AI-driven financial planning platforms that offer step-by-step guidance and recommendations based on clients' unique circumstances.
- AI-powered algorithms that analyse clients' spending patterns and provide personalised budgeting and savings advice.

Benefits:

- Improved client knowledge and understanding of financial concepts.

- Empowered clients who can make more informed financial decisions.
- Enhanced client-adviser relationship through personalised education and support.
- Increased client confidence and trust in their financial adviser.

Tailoring Educational Content to Clients' Preferences:

AI can help financial advisers understand clients' preferred learning styles and deliver educational content accordingly. By analysing client interactions and feedback, AI algorithms can identify the most effective communication channels, formats and frequencies for educational materials. This enables advisers to deliver educational content through mediums such as videos, podcasts, articles or interactive tools, catering to each client's unique preferences.

Examples:

- AI-powered platforms that track clients' engagement with educational content and recommend additional resources based on their interests.

- Personalised newsletters or email campaigns delivering educational insights based on clients' specific needs.

- AI chatbots that provide interactive quizzes or assessments to gauge clients' understanding of key financial concepts.

Benefits:

- Increased client engagement and participation in the educational process.

- Tailored educational content that aligns with clients' preferred learning styles.

- Efficient use of resources by focusing on content delivery channels that resonate with clients.

- Continuous feedback loop to improve and refine educational content over time.

Addressing knowledge gaps and supporting Consumer Duty:

AI can play a vital role in identifying and addressing clients' knowledge gaps in specific financial areas.

By analysing client data and interactions, AI algorithms can identify areas where clients may require additional education or clarification. This proactive approach not only empowers clients but also helps advisers meet their obligations under Consumer Duty by ensuring that clients have the necessary knowledge to make informed financial decisions.

Examples:

- AI-powered platforms that analyse clients' financial profiles and identify areas where educational interventions may be beneficial.
- Personalised AI-generated content addressing common misconceptions or frequently asked questions.
- AI chatbots that provide real-time explanations and educational resources during client-adviser interactions.

Benefits:

- Proactive identification and resolution of clients' knowledge gaps.

- Compliance with the Consumer Duty's requirement to enable and support customers in pursuing their financial objectives.
- Enhanced client satisfaction and trust in the advisory relationship.

Conclusion:

The integration of AI technologies in financial advisory businesses not only supports the principles of Consumer Duty but also revolutionises how financial advisers educate their clients.

By leveraging AI, advisers can deliver personalised educational content, tailor the learning experience to clients' preferences and bridge knowledge gaps to empower clients in making informed financial decisions. This strategic use of AI differentiates financial advisers by providing a value-added service that goes beyond traditional approaches. By embracing AI for client education, advisers can position themselves as forward-thinking professionals who prioritise client empowerment and engagement.

The benefits of leveraging AI for client education extend beyond compliance with the Consumer Duty. For example:

Competitive Advantage:

Financial advisers who adopt AI for client education gain a significant competitive advantage in the market. They can offer personalised, interactive and engaging educational experiences that set them apart from their peers. Clients are more likely to choose advisers who provide innovative and tailored educational resources to help them navigate complex financial matters. Indeed, clients who have experienced this level of service and value will be far more likely to make referrals and introductions to the advice firm.

Improved Client Outcomes:

AI-powered client education can lead to improved client outcomes. By enhancing clients' financial knowledge and understanding, advisers enable them to make well-informed decisions that align with their long-term goals. Empowered clients are more likely to make sound financial choices, ensuring their financial well-being and satisfaction.

Increased Efficiency:

AI streamlines the process of delivering educational content to clients. With AI-generated materials and automated systems, advisers can reach a larger audience while saving time and resources. AI platforms can provide clients with 24/7 access to educational resources, allowing them to learn at their own pace and convenience.

Personalisation at Scale:

AI enables advisers to deliver personalised educational experiences at scale. Through data analysis and machine learning algorithms, advisers can customise content based on clients' unique financial profiles, preferences and goals. This personalised approach fosters stronger client engagement and connection.

Continuous Improvement:

AI systems can continually analyse client interactions and feedback, allowing advisers to refine and improve their educational content. By understanding clients' evolving needs and preferences, advisers can adapt and update their educational resources accordingly. This iterative process ensures that educational content remains relevant, valuable and aligned with the dynamic nature of the financial landscape.

In conclusion, AI empowers financial advisers to meet the educational demands of

Consumer Duty while delivering an exceptional client experience.

Clearly, adoption of AI by financial planners in the UK will not be the be-all and end-all of meeting Consumer Duty requirements in itself, however, using AI for consumer education could nevertheless support financial planners' responsibilities in several ways. For example, AI could also help financial planners to:

- Provide clear and timely information to consumers about the products and services they offer, and how they align with consumers' needs and preferences.

- Monitor consumer outcomes and identify any potential risks or harms that may arise from their products or services.

- Engage with consumers in a fair and transparent manner and address any complaints or feedback promptly and effectively.

- Demonstrate that they have acted to deliver good consumer outcomes, and that they have put their customers' needs first.

By leveraging AI technologies, advisers can provide personalised, tailored and engaging educational content that equips clients with the knowledge and confidence to navigate their financial journeys successfully. This not only fulfils regulatory obligations but also drives client satisfaction, loyalty and long-term success.

Embracing AI for client education positions advisers at the forefront of industry innovation and sets the stage for a future-ready financial advisory practice.

Common Objections to AI

Addressing Concerns and Misconceptions

For many IFAs and advisers, the whole topic of AI is very much stepping into new territory, and it's normal and good to have concerns and reservations about this leap. After all, adopting a new technology, especially one as transformative as artificial intelligence, can feel like a monumental task.

This chapter is all about addressing concerns and worries - the *"What ifs"* that may be lingering in our minds. One thing is for sure, it's essential to approach AI with a clear understanding and a confident mindset, and that's what we're aiming for here.

Whether you're wondering about the complexity of AI, the cost, its impact on your role, or its compatibility with your business ethos, I've tried to cover a broad range of common objections that I have heard advisers raise over recent years and months. Having doubts doesn't mean you're resistant to change or behind the times - on the contrary, asking questions is critically important when dealing with matters such as clients' lives.

AI, with all its bells and whistles, is ultimately a tool to help you do your job 'better'.

And just like any tool, it's most effective when wielded by a skilled hand. Your expertise, judgment and personal touch remain paramount. AI is here to aid, not replace.

So, let's address some of these questions together, with an open mind and a focus on how we can shape AI to suit our unique needs. I hope that by the end of this chapter, you'll feel empowered to take the next step in this exciting AI journey.

All of the following are real concerns and 'objections' cited by financial advisers I have met at events and in person, followed by my response:

"AI is too complex for me to understand or use effectively."

It's very likely that some advisers will indeed feel overwhelmed by the technology. But what's important to know is that you don't need to be a tech expert to use AI. Many AI-based tools are designed with user-friendliness in mind, with simple interfaces and clear instructions. Plus, most vendors will offer training and support to help you learn how to use their tools effectively.

"AI will replace my job and make me redundant."

While AI can automate some tasks, it is primarily a tool to enhance your job, not replace it. AI can handle repetitive tasks, giving you more time to focus on complex activities that require human skills such as emotional intelligence, critical thinking and personal client relationships.

"AI is going to be expensive. I can't afford it."

It's a common misconception that AI is always costly. There are scalable options available that can fit within your budget. Besides, think of it as an investment; by automating routine tasks, you'll save time and resources, which can ultimately boost your productivity and profitability. Many AI tools are free to use.

"My clients prefer human interaction. AI can't replace that."

Absolutely, and it shouldn't! AI isn't about replacing human interaction; it's about enhancing it. AI can provide insights and analysis that help you serve your clients better, but it doesn't replace the personal touch you bring to your client relationships.

"I don't have the time to implement AI into my current processes."

It's true that introducing new tools into your workflow can take time, but many AI solutions are designed for easy integration with your existing systems. Plus, once set up, they can save you substantial time in the long run by automating time-consuming tasks. The purpose of this book is to help you get started on that integration process.

"AI is impersonal. I worry it could damage my client relationships."

It's all about how you use it. AI can be a fantastic tool for personalisation, helping you tailor your services to each client's needs based on data analysis. You remain at the forefront of the client relationship, with AI acting/serving as your support.

"AI can make mistakes, especially with complex financial decisions."

Like any tool, AI is not infallible. However, its algorithms are often more accurate than humans at processing vast amounts of data quickly. It's essential to use AI as an aid to decision-making, not the sole decision-maker, combining its quantitative analysis with your own qualitative judgment.

"AI might cause regulatory issues, as the giving of financial advice is a regulated activity."

At this stage, most financial advisers will not be allowing AI tools to give financial advice to their clients. As you will discover in this book, AI will primarily be used for a variety of other business processes to aid and enhance efficiencies.

"My business has been doing well without AI so far, so I don't see the need for it."

That's good to hear - however, AI isn't just about fixing problems; it's about finding new opportunities. AI can help you identify trends and insights you might miss, allowing you to offer more proactive and predictive services, which could set you apart from others and increase your business success. Most financial advice firms will, over time find their own unique ways to use AI which fit seamlessly into their business processes.

"Integrating AI may disrupt my established workflow and business process."

That's completely understandable, and change can often be unsettling, but the integration of AI is often a streamlined process involving rigorous testing. AI can also be phased in gradually, allowing your business to adjust without a major upheaval. The initial adjustment period is a small price to pay for the long-term efficiency gains. And again, AI isn't necessarily about fixing issues (that may not be broken anyway) – it is usually more about discovering new and more efficient ways of doing things.

"My team lacks the technical skills to operate AI tools."

You'd be surprised at how user-friendly AI tools have become! They are increasingly designed with non-technical users in mind. Plus, many AI providers offer extensive training and support to ensure your team feels comfortable and competent using their products.

"AI can't understand the subtleties of financial advising like a human can."

You're right that AI doesn't replicate human intuition and experience. However, it excels at tasks like data analysis, forecasting and generation reports and other written content. It's not about replacing the human touch but complementing it with powerful analytics and generative capabilities.

"The industry is changing rapidly. I worry the AI system will become outdated quickly."

It's true that technology evolves rapidly, but this is actually a strength of AI. Unlike traditional software that needs ‘manual’ updating, AI systems learn and adapt over time, often incorporating updates to reflect new trends, data and industry changes.

"I'm unsure of the ROI. It seems like a risky investment."

It's right and proper to be cautious about new investments. The ROI from AI comes from increased efficiency, improved accuracy, the ability to provide more personalised services and the speed at which it can create marketing and educational materials. While the benefits might not be immediate (though some aspects really are immediate), with time, the cost savings and potential for growth can make AI a worthy investment for your business.

~

I hope some of these answers have been of help, but if you have other questions or observations please don’t hesitate to get in touch.

Building your AI Roadmap

Eight Stages to Incorporating AI into your Financial Advice Business

Stage 1

Recognising the Need to Embrace AI and Appointing an AI Champion (up to 1 month)

The goal is to reach a consensus within the firm that adopting AI is necessary for future growth and efficiency. To begin, appoint an "AI Champion" who will be responsible for driving the AI initiative. This person will need to have the following attributes.

Attributes of the AI Champion:

- Tech-savvy: They should have a good understanding of AI and its potential applications, even if they're not an expert. A background in technology or a keen interest in AI could be beneficial.

- Influential: The AI Champion needs to be a person who can influence others in the firm. This could mean they are a senior leader, or simply a respected individual with the ability to gain buy-in from colleagues.

One option to consider is to appoint a non-executive director who takes on this role and who 'holds to account' and constructively challenges the leadership team, to make sure the project is completed.

- Strong communicator: They'll need to articulate the benefits of AI and explain complex concepts in a way that everyone in the firm can understand. They should also be able to address fears and uncertainties associated with AI adoption.

- Problem-solver: They should be good at identifying areas where AI could provide a solution or enhance efficiency. This means being familiar with the workings of the firm and having a good understanding of the challenges faced by financial advisers.

- Forward-thinking: They should be someone who can anticipate the future of the industry and understands the importance of staying ahead of the curve. They need to see the big picture of AI in the financial advisory industry.

- Resilient: AI adoption can face resistance and unforeseen hurdles along the way. The AI Champion needs to be someone who can navigate these obstacles and keep the project on track.

- Project Management Skills: The AI Champion will be effectively running a project that could span many months and indeed multiple years and involves many different components. Having strong project management skills will be vital.

At the outset of the AI adoption journey, it's essential for financial advice firms to acknowledge the need for embracing AI and appoint an AI Champion who will spearhead the AI initiative. This stage focuses on creating a consensus within the firm regarding the importance of AI adoption for future growth, efficiency and competitiveness.

By recognising the need to embrace AI and appointing an AI Champion with these attributes, financial advice firms can lay a strong foundation for their AI adoption journey. The AI Champion will play a central role in guiding the firm through the stages to come, ensuring a successful integration of AI into their operations.

Your Notes

Stage 2

Awareness and Education (1st to 3rd month)

The second milestone is for financial advisers to understand what AI is, its capabilities and how it is currently being used within financial services and elsewhere.

- Arrange webinars on AI and its impact on the finance industry.
- Enrol advisers in online courses focused on AI in finance.
- Share articles and white papers on AI in the finance industry.
- Debunk myths and fears about AI.
- Clearly communicate that AI is an amplification tool, not a replacement.

The second stage of the roadmap to AI adoption is centred around fostering awareness and education. It's crucial for financial advisers to gain a solid understanding of AI, its capabilities and how it's presently being utilised within the financial services industry and beyond. This stage lays the groundwork for successful AI adoption by demystifying the concept and providing an overview of its practical applications.

One of the key activities at this stage involves participating in or even arranging webinars focused on AI and its impact on the finance industry. These webinars can cover a range of topics, including current and potential uses of AI in finance, emerging trends and real-world case studies. They serve as platforms for thought leaders in AI and finance to share insights, spark discussions and answer any questions advisers might have.

The educational process can be supplemented by enrolling advisers in online courses that focus specifically on AI in finance. These courses can provide in-depth knowledge about AI, its types, its functioning and its relevance to financial advising. They help advisers gain not just theoretical knowledge but also practical insights that they can apply in their work.

Another component of this stage is sharing informative content such as articles, white papers and research reports on AI in the finance industry. Reading such materials can help advisers stay updated with the latest AI trends, understand the different perspectives on AI in finance and learn about successful AI adoption practices. It will only be a matter of time until there are a plethora of podcasts around the topic that will be of value to advisers.

Moreover, it's important to debunk myths and fears about AI at this stage. There's a common misconception that AI might* replace human jobs, which can create resistance towards its adoption. It's crucial to dispel these fears and emphasise that AI is an amplification tool, not a replacement. It's about enhancing the adviser's capabilities, providing them with valuable insights, helping them serve their clients better and allowing them to focus on the more strategic and human aspects of their roles.

In summary, the Awareness and Education stage is all about equipping financial advisers with the knowledge and understanding they need to be comfortable with AI, see its value and be ready to leverage its capabilities in their work.

*Of course, it would be disingenuous to suggest that AI will *never* replace some roles within the profession, and there are various schools of thought as to how and when this might happen.

The question of whether artificial intelligence will fully replace financial planners, IFAs and financial advisers is not easy to answer. AI has the potential to revolutionise many aspects of the financial industry, such as portfolio management, marketing and communications, data analysis and customer service. It can also provide valuable insights and recommendations based on large datasets and complex algorithms, however AI is not yet capable of replicating the human element of financial advising, such as providing personalised advice and support to clients based on their unique financial situation and goals.

AI also lacks the human expertise and judgement that financial advisers bring to the table, such as an understanding of financial markets, products and strategies. Indeed, clients may be hesitant to trust a machine with their financial decisions, especially when it comes to complex or high-stakes issues.

So while AI will undoubtedly play a major role in the financial advisory industry going forward, it's unlikely that it will completely replace human financial advisers in the near future.

The whole point of this book is to help financial advisers prepare themselves **by adapting their businesses and leveraging the opportunities that AI brings**.

Indeed some advisers are already finding AI to be remarkably helpful in their businesses. Here's what one told me recently:

"Hi Phil. As you are aware, I have been using AI quite a bit recently.

I have been using it to provide base material for my client newsletters and it has provided me with documents about behavioural investing and the benefits of financial life planning.

I have used it for PowerPoint slides and for creating historic returns tables for treasury bonds and the S&P 500 since 1926.

I have also used it to extrapolate and summarise important points from large documents and to create a personal financial planning template.

I've just built an attitude to volatility, not risk questionnaire with point scoring system and overviews. Mind blown."

Mike LeGassick, Financial Planner and behavioural Investment Coach

Another IFA Martin Dodd of the Midlands Investment Agency posted this in our AI Best Practice Group:

"I asked ChatGPT to write a suitability report. This was after a single prompt and no data.

Imagine what it could do if you provide more prompts.

SUITABILITY REPORT FOR FINANCIAL ADVISER

Introduction:

This suitability report has been prepared for the benefit of Mr. John Smith, a potential client of ABC Financial Services. The report has been prepared based on the information provided by the client in his fact-find document and after a thorough analysis of his financial situation, objectives, and needs.

Investment Objectives:

Mr. Smith's primary investment objective is to achieve capital growth over the long term to fund his retirement in 25 years' time. He is willing to accept a moderate level of risk to achieve his objective.

Investment Experience:

Mr. Smith has previous experience investing in mutual funds and stocks through a self-directed brokerage account. He understands the risks associated with investing in the stock market and has indicated a willingness to take on some level of risk to achieve his investment objectives.

Risk Tolerance:

Based on Mr. Smith's responses in his fact-find document, his risk tolerance is moderate. He is willing to accept some level of risk to achieve his investment objectives, but he also has a need for stability in his investment portfolio.

Investment Recommendations:

After a thorough analysis of Mr. Smith's financial situation and investment objectives, we recommend the following investments:

Balanced mutual funds with exposure to stocks and bonds. This will provide Mr. Smith with the potential for capital growth while also offering some level of stability to his portfolio.

Blue-chip stocks with a history of consistent dividend payments. These stocks provide a potential for capital growth and also offer a regular income stream through dividend payments.

Fixed-income securities such as government bonds or corporate bonds. These investments offer stability and regular income payments.

Conclusion:

Based on our analysis of Mr. Smith's financial situation and investment objectives, we believe that the recommended investments are suitable for him. We have taken into consideration his investment experience, risk tolerance, and need for stability in his portfolio. We believe that these investments will help Mr. Smith achieve his long-term investment objectives while also managing his risk appropriately. As with any investment, there is always the potential for loss, and we recommend that Mr. Smith reviews his portfolio regularly to ensure that it remains aligned with his investment objectives and risk tolerance.

"A very interesting result!" concluded Martin.

Your Notes

Stage 3

Exploration and Identification (3rd to 6th month)

- Identify areas in the financial advisory process where AI can add value.
- Brainstorm how AI can solve problems or enhance efficiency in adviser roles.
- Foster discussions on AI use cases within your specific organisation.

As you transition into the third stage of AI adoption, the focus shifts from understanding the general concept of AI to exploring its specific applications within your financial advisory process. The objective here is to identify areas where AI can add value, solve problems, enhance efficiency and ultimately drive your business's growth.

Note: At the time of writing, it's still quite early days in the adoption of AI technologies within the world of financial advice, and whilst we have a pretty clear view of direction of travel, it will take time to 'bed in' within most financial advice businesses, for example with readymade solutions. The point of this book is to provide a roadmap for when AI is more widely available throughout the profession – but trust me, that will be sooner than you think.

As a rough guide, here are some of the ways AI can notionally be used now by financial advisers:

Automated Data Analysis: AI can analyse client data and financial markets to provide insights and predictions that can support financial decisions. This analysis can include trend identification, risk assessments and investment opportunity identification.

Robo-Advisers: These automated platforms use algorithms to provide financial advice or investment management online with minimal human intervention – perhaps if you want to explore different markets for your business to target. They can provide lower-cost financial advice solutions, particularly for less complex financial situations.

Customer Relationship Management (CRM): AI-integrated CRM systems can track customer interactions, predict customer needs and behaviour, and provide personalised communication to improve client relationships.

Compliance and Regulatory Requirements: AI can be used to monitor transactions and ensure that financial planning activities comply with legal and regulatory requirements. This includes flagging any suspicious activities, automatically generating required reports, and providing updates on regulatory changes.

Automated Report Generation: AI can assist in automatically generating client reports based on data analysis, significantly reducing the time spent on these tasks by human staff.

Chatbots for Customer Service: Chatbots can provide instant, 24/7 support for simple client inquiries, booking appointments or directing clients to the right team member for their needs.

Chatbots for Business Processes: Adviser firms with detailed documented processes can create chatbots which enable members of staff to rapidly access information on specific processes in any number of different scenarios.

Marketing Materials: We'll cover this in more detail later, but Generative AI can be used in a variety of different ways to create marketing content and materials, much of which can be highly personalised to specific target markets and niches.

And as for three to five years down the line:

Predictive Behavioural Analytics: More advanced AI algorithms could predict client behaviours and financial market trends with increased accuracy, using not only structured financial data but also unstructured data from various sources like social media.

Advanced Personalised Financial Planning: AI systems could offer highly personalised financial advice based on a client's financial situation, personal values, lifestyle and goals. This could involve a deeper understanding of each client and the ability to adjust plans in real time as situations change.

Automated Financial Coaching: AI could provide ongoing, real-time financial coaching to clients. This could include AI-powered apps that offer instant financial advice and learning resources tailored to a client's personal financial situation and objectives.

Intelligent Document Analysis: AI could analyse various financial documents, extract and summarise the important information, and even suggest appropriate actions based on the data.

Proactive Compliance Management: Future AI systems might predict potential compliance issues before they arise, making it easier to proactively manage regulatory requirements.

Real-time Risk Assessment: AI could continually monitor and evaluate the risk level of client portfolios, considering a wider range of factors and making real-time adjustments based on market fluctuations and changes in a client's personal situation.

The number of software providers offering AI capabilities for financial advice firms will grow rapidly over the coming years, and the choices you make will clearly depend on specific needs, budget and existing infrastructure. Hence the need for having an AI Champion in your business as described earlier.

Stage 3 continued.

This stage begins by conducting a comprehensive review of the financial advisory process, with the aim of pinpointing areas where AI can be applied for optimisation. Whether it's automating routine tasks, providing advanced data analytics, personalising client interactions or detecting potentially fraudulent activities, AI can offer several advantages. This process of identification should take into account the unique characteristics of your business, your clients' needs and your team's capabilities.

The next step is to brainstorm how AI can resolve existing challenges or boost efficiency in adviser roles. By fostering an open and creative dialogue, you can uncover innovative ways to leverage AI that align with your firm's goals and objectives. For instance, AI could automate administrative tasks, freeing up advisers to spend more time on client interaction. Or AI-driven analytics could provide deeper insights into market trends, assisting advisers in making more informed decisions.

In addition, it's important to facilitate discussions on AI use cases within your specific organisation. By encouraging your team to share ideas and perspectives, you can collaboratively identify potential AI projects that have a high chance of success. These discussions should also involve stakeholders from different levels of the organisation to ensure a holistic understanding of where and how AI can be implemented effectively.

This stage of Exploration and Identification forms the basis for a strategic approach to AI adoption. It helps align AI initiatives with your firm's needs and capabilities, ensuring that AI doesn't just become a buzzword but a tool that brings tangible benefits to your business and clients.

Your Notes

Stage 4

Planning and Prioritising (6th to 9th month)

- Prioritise AI opportunities based on potential impact, cost of implementation, readiness of technology, etc.
- Create a phased strategy for AI implementation.
- Determine necessary resources and potential vendors for AI solutions.

Upon entering the fourth stage of AI adoption, you're ready to take the findings from your exploration and identification efforts and turn them into a concrete, actionable plan. This phase is all about making strategic decisions on which AI opportunities to pursue based on a range of criteria and laying out a clear, phased strategy for implementation.

One of the first steps in this stage is to prioritise AI opportunities. The aim is to rank the identified AI applications according to factors such as:

- The potential impact on the business
- The cost of implementation
- Readiness of the technology, and

- The firm's capacity to integrate and manage the AI solution.

This ranking will help determine which opportunities should be pursued first, based on the balance between their potential benefits and the resources required.

After determining the priorities, it's time to create a phased strategy for AI implementation. This involves designing a roadmap that outlines the sequence of AI integrations, with detailed timelines and milestones. A phased approach allows for careful management of resources, provides room for learning and adjustments along the way and helps ensure a smoother transition for the staff and operations.

Simultaneously, it's crucial to identify the necessary resources and potential vendors for AI solutions. Assess your current resources, including personnel, technology and budget and determine what additional resources are needed. As for choosing vendors, consider factors such as their expertise, reliability, cost and the alignment of their solutions with your specific requirements.

In essence, the planning and prioritising stage involves making strategic decisions and laying a solid foundation for AI implementation. By the end of this stage, your firm should have a clear plan of action, with identified resources and vendors, ready to kickstart the AI integration process.

Your Notes

Stage 5

Pilot Testing (9th to 12th month)

- Implement AI in one or two priority areas.
- Monitor the effectiveness of the implemented AI solution.
- Make necessary adjustments based on feedback and the observed effectiveness.

Stage 5, Pilot Testing, marks the beginning of the AI implementation process. However, instead of going all-in at once, the idea is to first implement AI in one or two priority areas. By doing so, you have the opportunity to observe the technology in action, identify any teething issues and assess its effectiveness on a smaller scale before a wider deployment.

The first step in this stage is to select one or two areas that have been identified as high priority during the Planning and Prioritising stage. This might be an area where AI has the potential to create significant efficiencies or solve a specific challenge that your firm has been grappling with. Once these areas are selected, you can work with your chosen vendor or your in-house team to integrate the AI solution.

After the AI solution has been implemented, it's crucial to monitor its effectiveness closely. This involves tracking key performance indicators (KPIs) that were identified in the Planning and Prioritising stage. These KPIs may relate to efficiency, accuracy, cost savings or other aspects that align with the goals for your AI adoption.

Additionally, it's important to collect feedback from end-users, whether they're your advisers, support staff or clients. They can provide invaluable insights into the solution's functionality, usability and impact on their work.

The final part of this stage is to make necessary adjustments based on feedback and observed effectiveness. This may involve tweaking the AI solution or modifying how it's used. The flexibility to refine the solution at this stage is one of the benefits of pilot testing.

In summary, the Pilot Testing stage is about taking the first steps in AI implementation, learning from these initial experiences and refining the solution to maximise its effectiveness. By the end of this stage, your firm should be well-equipped with knowledge and insights to scale up the AI integration across other areas of the business.

Your Notes

Stage 6

Evaluation and Adjustment (12th to 18th month)

- Evaluate the results of the pilot phase.
- Collect feedback from both clients and advisers on the AI implementation.
- Fine-tune your approach based on feedback and learnings from the pilot phase.

Following the initial phase of implementation, the Evaluation and Adjustment stage begins. The first step of this stage is to evaluate the results of the pilot phase. This involves assessing the performance of the AI implementation against the set KPIs and goals defined in the Planning and Prioritising stage. The objective is to gauge whether the AI solution has met or exceeded expectations, brought the desired efficiencies and resolved the identified challenges.

Collecting feedback is a critical part of this stage. This feedback should come from a range of stakeholders including advisers who are using the AI system and clients who may be experiencing the effects of the AI implementation indirectly. Feedback can provide insights into user satisfaction, system usability and potential areas of improvement that may not be visible through quantitative assessment alone. It also helps in understanding the AI system's impact on client relationships and service delivery.

Based on the results of the evaluation and the feedback collected, adjustments to the AI implementation strategy may be required. This could involve fine-tuning the AI system, refining workflows, providing additional training, or even reconsidering the choice of AI applications if the current one does not yield the expected results. This stage underlines the iterative nature of AI implementation, where learnings from each cycle are used to continuously improve the system and strategy.

By the end of the Evaluation and Adjustment stage, your firm should have a clear understanding of the benefits and challenges of the implemented AI solution, a refined AI strategy and a well-informed approach to expand AI integration into other areas of your operations.

Your Notes

Stage 7

Rollout and Expansion (18th to 24th month)

- Expand the AI features across more areas based on the success of the pilot phase.
- Solicit and incorporate feedback as you expand AI capabilities.

On entering Stage 7, Rollout and Expansion, your firm will have gained a robust understanding of AI's utility within its operations and be ready for a more extensive implementation. Having validated the success of the AI solution in the pilot phase, you can now confidently roll it out across multiple facets of the business.

The beginning of this stage involves expanding the AI features across more areas of the business. This might mean introducing AI-driven analytics to a broader range of departments, using AI to optimise more workflows, or implementing AI features that enhance more areas of customer service. The knowledge and insights gained from the previous stages will guide you in selecting which areas will most benefit from AI integration.

However, this is not a process of merely duplicating what worked in the pilot phase. Each area of your business is unique and might have specific needs and considerations that weren't present in the initial pilot area. It's important to tailor the AI implementation to the specific requirements and context of each new area.

As with previous stages, feedback collection remains an essential part of the Rollout and Expansion stage. As the AI features are expanded, continuous feedback from users – both advisers and clients – should be requested. This will allow you to monitor user satisfaction, identify any potential issues early and fine-tune the AI solutions as necessary.

The goal is to incorporate this feedback and the learnings from the pilot phase, to continually improve the AI implementation. It's a process of constant learning, adjustment and improvement – the AI journey doesn't stop with this stage but continues as an ongoing part of the firm's operations.

In essence, the Rollout and Expansion stage is about leveraging the knowledge and successes from the pilot phase to integrate AI into the wider business, continually refining the implementation based on feedback and changing needs and solidifying AI as an integral part of your firm's strategy and operations.

Your Notes

Stage 8

Continuous Learning and Updating (24th month onwards)

- Stay updated with latest AI advancements in the industry.
- Foster an environment of continuous learning and innovation.
- Encourage advisers to proactively find new ways to apply AI in their practice.

Remember, training and change management are integral to each stage, ensuring your advisers are not just familiar with, but also comfortable using the new AI systems and tools.

Stage 8 marks the culmination of the AI adoption journey, but it also signifies a new beginning - a commitment to continuous learning, growth and innovation. In this stage, you embrace a mindset of staying updated with the latest AI advancements, fostering a culture of continuous learning and encouraging advisers to proactively seek new ways to apply AI in their practice.

To stay at the forefront of AI advancements, it's crucial to actively monitor the industry landscape. Keep a pulse on emerging trends, breakthrough technologies and best practices related to AI in financial advising. This could involve attending industry conferences, participating in AI-focused webinars or workshops and following reputable sources that provide insights into the evolving AI landscape.

By staying updated, you can identify new opportunities, anticipate challenges and adapt your AI strategy accordingly. Clearly this will be a key role for not just your AI Champion, but most key people within the business.

Creating an environment of continuous learning and innovation is essential for sustained AI success. Encourage your team to engage in ongoing education and professional development opportunities related to AI and its applications in the financial advising realm. This might include providing access to AI training programs, organising internal knowledge-sharing sessions, or even fostering collaborative partnerships with AI experts or academic institutions. By investing in your team's growth, you empower them to explore new possibilities and embrace a culture of innovation.

Additionally, foster a culture where, within the normal boundaries of privacy, data protection and compliance, advisers are encouraged to proactively explore and experiment with AI in their practice. Encourage them to identify new use cases, propose innovative solutions and share their insights and learnings with their colleagues. Emphasise the importance of embracing a growth mindset and being open to exploring uncharted territories. By tapping into the collective knowledge and creativity of your team, you can unlock new avenues for leveraging AI and drive continuous improvement in your advisory services.

In summary, Stage 8 is about recognising that the journey of AI adoption is ongoing. By embracing continuous learning, staying informed about the latest advancements, fostering a culture of innovation and encouraging proactive exploration by your advisers, you position your firm to remain at the cutting edge of AI in financial advising and planning. This commitment to ongoing learning and updating ensures that your AI initiatives continue to evolve and deliver tangible benefits to your firm and clients in the ever-changing landscape of AI.

Your Notes

Managing Change During AI Adoption

Facing the AI Headwinds

Adopting AI is a substantial change that touches various aspects of a financial advice firm, from internal processes to client interactions. Such a change, while beneficial in the long term, can be challenging to implement. It is crucial to consider change management principles to ensure a smooth transition.

1. Communication:

Transparency is key in any change process. Start by communicating the reasons for the change, the benefits expected and how it will impact everyone's roles. The goal is not just to inform but to create a dialogue. Encourage questions and feedback to address concerns and misunderstandings promptly. The AI Champion can play a critical role in facilitating this communication.

2. Training:

Invest in adequate training for your employees to get them comfortable with the new AI systems. The training should be tailored to different roles to ensure it's relevant. And it's not just about technical training; soft skills training to help employees adapt to the change may also be necessary.

3. Leadership Involvement:

Senior leadership should actively support the change, as their commitment signals the importance of the change to the rest of the firm. They should be visibly involved, for instance, by participating in training or regularly updating the team on the project's progress.

4. Pilot Testing:

Introducing change gradually often works better than a complete overhaul. Pilot testing allows employees to get comfortable with the new systems in a controlled setting and provides an opportunity to tweak the system based on feedback before a full rollout.

5. Employee Involvement:

Involving employees in the change process, for example, by seeking their input on potential AI applications, can increase their sense of ownership and buy-in.

6. Celebrating Successes:

Recognise and celebrate milestones, even small ones, along the way. This helps maintain morale and shows progress, making the change feel less daunting.

7. Continuous Improvement:

Once the change has been implemented, continue to monitor the outcomes and make adjustments as needed. Treat the change as an ongoing process, not a one-off project.

Summary

- Maintain transparent communication about the reasons for the change, its benefits and its impact.
- Provide adequate and role-specific training for all employees.
- Ensure senior leadership is visibly supportive and involved in the change.
- Introduce change gradually, starting with pilot testing.
- Involve employees in the change process to foster a sense of ownership.
- Recognise and celebrate milestones to maintain morale.
- Treat the change as an ongoing process and continue to make adjustments post-implementation.

Your Notes

Other Important Considerations

Beyond the Horizon of AI Integration

Introducing new technology into your business with the goal of creating greater efficiencies and value for clients is one thing; considering how it impacts wider aspects of the business is also critical.

Let's look at some of them.

Ethical Considerations of AI

AI is not just a technological transformation; it has ethical implications as well. How is client data used and protected? How does AI affect employment within the industry? Discussing these ethical questions with your team and key stakeholders will be key to your AI journey. It is essential that everyone is on the same page when it comes to ethical considerations.

Regulatory Compliance

The financial industry is highly regulated and using AI brings its own legal and compliance considerations. It goes without saying that involvement of your Compliance professionals will need to be central to your AI journey.

As one senior IFA once told me: *"Over many years in the industry, I've learnt the hard way that Compliance people don't like surprises"*.

Cybersecurity

With an increased reliance on technology and data, the risk of cyber threats also grows. Exploring best practices in AI-related cybersecurity will also be important.

Case Studies and Examples

Real-world examples of AI usage in the financial advice industry should be sought out wherever possible. These can be particularly effective within the stages covering Exploration and Identification, Pilot Testing and Rollout and Expansion.

Risk Management

As AI systems become integral to operations, the business risks associated with system failure increase. How these risks can be managed should be carefully considered.

Costs and ROI

Implementing AI at a deep and integrated level can be expensive, though some use of AI within a financial advice business can actually be free (e.g. ChatGPT basic). A financial analysis of AI investment, including expected costs, potential savings and return on investment (ROI), will be beneficial.

Client Perspectives

How might clients react to the increased use of AI in financial advising? Some clients might be thrilled with the efficiencies and capabilities, while others might be concerned about the impersonal nature of AI. Addressing these potential reactions should be considered, along with the different ways you will inform clients of your plans.

As financial planners, you have a responsibility to provide fair and suitable advice to your clients, especially those who are vulnerable or have additional needs. The FCA's new Consumer Duty sets out clear expectations for firms to act in the best interests of their customers and deliver good outcomes for them. One of the key aspects of the Consumer Duty is to pay attention to the needs of customers with characteristics of vulnerability, who may be at greater risk of harm or have difficulties making informed decisions.

In your AI journey, you will need to consider how to use technology to enhance your service and value proposition for vulnerable clients, without compromising on quality or compliance.

For example, you may want to use AI tools to help you identify and segment vulnerable clients, tailor your communications, products and services to their preferences and needs, monitor their outcomes and feedback, and provide them with additional support or guidance when needed.

You will also need to ensure that your AI systems are transparent, fair, accurate and secure, and that you have appropriate governance and oversight mechanisms in place.

Your Notes

AI Skills Needed

Unlocking the Secrets of Digital Expertise

Clearly, adoption of AI by individual financial advisers and advice firms will require some new skills, expertise and proficiencies. Below are some key skills and abilities that someone would typically need in order to use AI at an **advanced** level – perhaps for a large financial advice firm that intends to go 'all in'.

Understanding of Data Analytics:

The backbone of AI is data. Understanding how to analyse, interpret and manipulate data is crucial. This includes skills in statistics and probability.

Example: Being able to analyse customer financial data to find trends and patterns that can be used to create better financial plans.

Data Visualisation:

The ability to visualise data helps to understand patterns, trends and to communicate AI results effectively.

Example: Using tools like Tableau or PowerBI to create visualisations of a client's projected financial growth based on different investment strategies.

Data Pre-processing:

AI algorithms need clean data to function effectively. Understanding how to pre-process data, such as dealing with missing values or outliers, is crucial.

Example: Cleaning financial data from various sources to ensure that AI tools can use it effectively.

Basic Understanding of Machine Learning Algorithms:

While it's not necessary to be able to code these algorithms from scratch, having a basic understanding of how they work, their strengths and weaknesses, and which to use in a given scenario is important.

Example: Knowing when to use a linear regression model versus a neural network for a particular financial forecasting task.

What's this mean? Deciding between a linear regression model and a neural network for finance predictions is like choosing between a simple and a complex tool. Linear regression, the simpler tool, can help understand how one thing impacts another, like how changing interest rates might change house prices.

On the other hand, a neural network, the complex tool, can handle lots of factors at once. For example, it can predict house prices based on multiple things like interest rates, location, and size all together. It's used for trickier problems where many factors work together in not-so-clear ways.

Programming Skills:

Some level of programming skills is often necessary to work effectively with AI. Python and R are commonly used languages in the field.

Example: Writing a Python script to automate data collection or analysis.

Ethical Use of AI:

Understanding the ethical implications of AI use is important. This includes issues of data privacy, bias in AI algorithms, and more.

Example: Ensuring that client data is used ethically and responsibly when training AI models.

Communication Skills:

Being able to explain complex AI concepts in simple terms is crucial. This is especially important when dealing with stakeholders who may not be familiar with AI.

Example: Explaining to clients how an AI-based tool is managing their investments and what its recommendations are based on.

Critical Thinking:

The ability to critically evaluate AI output, understand its limitations, and apply it in the most effective way.

Example: Not taking the output of a financial forecasting model at face value but understanding its limitations based on the data it was trained on.

Project Management Skills:

Implementing AI can be a complex process that requires careful planning, coordination of different resources, and managing timelines.

Example: Effectively managing the implementation of a new AI tool in a financial advisory firm.

Understanding of Domain Knowledge:

Applying AI effectively requires a deep understanding of the domain in which it's being applied. In the case of financial advisers, this means understanding finance, investments, risk management, etc.

Example: Using an understanding of financial markets to make better decisions about how to use AI in financial planning.

Remember, while these skills are beneficial, not everyone in a team needs to have all of them! It's often more effective to have a diverse team with different skill sets when working with AI.

Skills Needed by Smaller Advice Firms

For smaller businesses or even a one-person financial advice firm, it's key to focus on the most impactful skills that can be self-taught or learned without a heavy time investment. Here are three fundamental skills:

Basic Understanding of Data Analytics:

Grasping the fundamentals of data analytics is critical for making the most out of AI tools. This doesn't mean becoming a data scientist, but rather understanding basic concepts like data sorting, filtering and understanding simple patterns in data.

Example: Learning to organise and filter client data, identify patterns, or interpret the output from your AI tools can lead to better and more efficient decision making.

Ethical Use of AI:

As a financial adviser, it's crucial to understand how to use AI ethically. This includes being aware of how data is being used, what data privacy means, and ensuring the AI tools are being used responsibly.

Example: Learning about data privacy laws and ethical guidelines for AI use in financial services and making sure your AI tools comply with these.

Communicating AI concepts:

As a financial adviser, you don't just need to understand AI - you also need to be able to explain it to your clients in simple, accessible terms. They may have questions about how AI is impacting their financial planning, and it's your job to help them understand.

Example: Learning to explain in simple terms how your AI tools help with tasks like market analysis or investment suggestions can build trust with your clients.

With these three skills, a small financial advice business can make effective use of AI tools while ensuring ethical use and clear communication with clients. There are a variety of online courses, workshops, and other resources available that can help you build these skills at your own pace. YouTube is your friend here, as well as LinkedIn's Learning hub.

Your Notes

Using AI for Marketing

Getting Stuff Done

Imagine that you are starting up a financial advice firm from scratch. You're excited about your new business and have grand plans.

Quite apart from everything else that you'll need to do to get going, you reach 'Marketing' on your to-do list. And if you ask Google or an industry consultant to come up with a full menu of marketing collateral that your financial advice business might need, they will probably come up with a list like this (in no particular order):

1. Marketing Strategy and Plan
2. Company Brochure
3. Brand Guidelines
4. Logo
5. Fact Sheets
6. Flyers
7. Local Newspaper and Online Advertisements
8. Directory Listings
9. Case Studies and Client Testimonials
10. Monthly/Quarterly Market Reports
11. Client Newsletters

12. White Papers and Special Reports
13. Website Content
14. Articles and Blogs
15. Business Cards
16. Company Presentation/Deck
17. Seminar and Webinar Content and Slide Decks
18. Seminar and Webinar Invitations
19. Email Templates
20. Professional Referral Letters and Emails
21. Social Media Strategy
22. Social Media Posts
23. Podcast
24. Educational and Explainer Videos
25. Infographics
26. Press Release Templates
27. Client Onboarding Documents
28. Pricing and Fees descriptions
29. Client Personas
30. Website Chatbot
31. Online Quizzes and Scorecards
32. Search Engine Optimisation (SEO) Keywords
33. Client Surveys
34. eBooks, eGuides and Lead Magnets
35. Your own App
36. Checklists and FAQs

Clearly, they're not *all* essential, but the main objective of these collateral documents is to inform potential (and existing) clients about your firm's services, qualities and expertise - which in turn will establish trust and credibility and persuade them to engage with you or refer you to others.

As a list, it's quite daunting, and you begin to wonder if you have sufficient budget…

Cue Generative AI – the most well-known of which is currently ChatGPT. And what many advisers don't realise is that **every single item on this list can be created, for free, and in seconds using ChatGPT**.

Examples

Let's put ChatGPT to the test and ask it to create three items from the list – starting with a **Social Media plan**.

Firstly, here's a prompt you might use in ChatGPT. Vary it to suit your own needs and don't be afraid to be even more detailed.

Prompt:

"Write a comprehensive social media strategy and plan for my financial planning business. I'm based near Guildford in Surrey, and whilst I target business owners who are approximately five years from retirement, I also have a number of surgeons as clients who work in London. My social media plan needs to reach these types of prospects and create curiosity in my services. The tone needs to be professional but engaging, and these prospects need to feel that I am 'speaking' directly to them. Include tactics and timescales."

Output:

Social Media Strategy for Jones & Co Financial Planning

I. Overview

This social media strategy is designed to increase your visibility and credibility among business owners near retirement and surgeons in the London area. The goal is to engage these audiences, establish trust, and promote Jones & Co in a professional yet engaging manner.

II. Target Audience

1. Business owners in Surrey who are approximately five years from retirement.

2. Surgeons in London.

III. Key Social Media Platforms

1. LinkedIn: As the premier professional social networking platform, LinkedIn will be the primary vehicle for reaching your target audience.

2. Facebook: As the most widely used social media platform, Facebook provides an opportunity to reach a broader audience.

3. Instagram: Instagram, though less professional in nature, can help you connect with your audience on a personal level.

IV. Tactics

LinkedIn

- Content Creation: Post weekly updates discussing financial planning topics specifically relevant to pre-retirees and medical professionals. This might include retirement planning, wealth management, tax efficiency, pensions, etc.

- Networking: Connect and engage with local business groups, medical professional groups, and individuals fitting your client profile. Comment on their posts and share relevant articles to your network.

- Sponsored Content: Consider sponsored posts or LinkedIn ads to reach a broader audience outside of your network.

- Thought Leadership: Publish bi-monthly articles to position yourself as a thought leader. Topics might include unique financial considerations for business owners/surgeons, retirement readiness, or financial wellbeing.

Facebook

- Facebook Page: Maintain a Facebook business page with regular updates and posts related to your services.

- Groups: Participate in local business owner and medical professional groups, offering expert advice and commentary.
- Ads: Consider using Facebook's advanced targeting tools to reach your specific demographic.

Instagram

- Posts/Stories: Share images and short videos showing a "day in the life" at your office or brief snippets of financial education. Leverage Instagram stories for real-time updates.
- Influencer Collaboration: Connect with influencers who cater to your audience. For instance, lifestyle influencers who focus on the 'retirement life' or health/medical influencers in the London area.

V. Content Themes

1. Financial Planning 101: Basic concepts in a simple and understandable way.

2. Niche Financial Advice: Tailored advice for pre-retirees and medical professionals.

3. Client Success Stories: Stories from clients who have benefited from your services.

4. Behind-the-scenes: Show your office environment, team members, and events.

VI. Timeframes

LinkedIn: Weekly updates (every Monday), bi-monthly articles (1st and 3rd week of the month), daily networking.

Facebook: Weekly posts (every Wednesday), daily group interactions, monthly ad campaigns.

Instagram: Bi-weekly posts/stories, monthly influencer collaborations.

VII. Monitoring and Evaluation

Use social media analytics to track engagement (likes, shares, comments), reach, and conversions to website visits or inquiries.

Review strategy quarterly to adjust tactics based on performance.

Conduct a yearly review to assess overall success and set new goals.

Remember, social media success takes time and consistency. Be patient, and with persistent effort, you'll be able to build a strong online presence for Jones & Co.

As a first draft, this is pretty good; in fact if you have never written a social media plan before, this is good to go, at least for Jones & Co. As mentioned before, this is 'the cake' – you can now add the icing by tweaking and adjusting the output. If you want more detail on a particular section, just ask the AI to expand on what it has created.

Now let's create **client personas** for the same business. First, what is a client persona and why is it important?

A client persona is a fictional representation of your ideal client based on market research and data about your existing clients. It helps you to understand their needs, goals, challenges, preferences and behaviours. A client persona can help you tailor your financial planning services and marketing strategies to attract and retain more clients who fit your criteria.

Creating client personas is important for financial planners because it allows you to segment your market and target your messages much more effectively. By knowing who your ideal clients are, you can communicate with them in a way that resonates with them and addresses their particular pain points. You can also design your services to meet their specific needs and expectations. Client personas can also help you increase your conversion rates, client satisfaction, loyalty and of course, referrals.

Prompt:

"Now create client personas based on my previous input".

Output:

Client Persona 1: The Pre-Retirement Business Owner

Name: John

Age: 60

Occupation: Owns a successful manufacturing company based in Guildford, Surrey.

Family: Married with two grown-up children, one of whom works in the family business.

Goals:

- John is aiming to retire within the next five years and wants to ensure he has a robust financial plan in place.
- He wants to ensure the smooth transition of his business to his daughter.
- He also wishes to maintain his current lifestyle post-retirement, travel more, and potentially invest in a holiday home abroad.

Challenges:

- Uncertain about how to plan his finances for retirement.

- Concerned about the potential tax implications of passing on his business to his children.
- Needs guidance on balancing his spending between his lifestyle desires and leaving a legacy.

Social Media Habits:

- Active on LinkedIn, where he networks with other business owners and follows industry trends.
- Occasionally uses Facebook and Instagram to connect with friends and family.

Client Persona 2: The Surgeon

Name: Dr. Emily

Age: 45

Occupation: Senior surgeon at a prominent London hospital.

Family: Single, no children.

Goals:

- Emily is financially well off but is too busy to manage her finances effectively.
- She aims to maximise her investments to fund an early retirement.
- She also wants to ensure she's making the most of her high income while mitigating her tax liabilities.

Challenges:

- Has little time to devote to financial planning due to her demanding job.
- Uncertain about the best investment strategies for her high-income bracket.
- Concerned about maintaining her lifestyle post-retirement, given she has no dependents.

Social Media Habits:

- Active on LinkedIn, where she follows medical developments and engages with colleagues.
- Uses Instagram for leisure, following travel and lifestyle influencers.
- Has a Facebook account but isn't very active.

Again, pretty good for a first draft. You can make your personas even more detailed if you wish, simply by asking the AI to expand on different aspects.

Finally, let's now invite the pre-retirement business owner and others like him to a local seminar.

Prompt:

"I want to host a free educational seminar on retirement planning for pre-retirement business owners in Guildford and wider Surrey area. The venue will be Denbies Vineyard in Dorking and it will be on the afternoon of Saturday 27th May at 2pm for a maximum of two hours. Write a professional but friendly invitation to the seminar, highlighting several benefits of attending, one of which will be that they will meet other business owners in the area. There will also be a free wine tasting after the seminar. Provide different ways for people to RSVP."

Output:

Dear John,

As a fellow business owner and financial planner, I know how important it is to plan for your future. That's why I'm inviting you to a free educational seminar on retirement planning for business owners in Guildford and wider Surrey area.

The seminar will cover topics such as:

- How to maximise your pension savings and tax benefits
- How to diversify your income sources and reduce your risk exposure
- How to create a retirement lifestyle that suits your goals and preferences

We will also share real case studies and you will have ample time to ask questions.

The seminar will be held at Denbies Vineyard in Dorking on Saturday 27th May at 2pm. It will last for a maximum of two hours, followed by a free wine tasting session.

This is a great opportunity to learn from our team of experts, network with other business owners in the area, and enjoy some delicious wine.

To reserve your spot, please RSVP by one of the following methods:

- Call me at 01234 567890

- Email me at name@email.com
- Fill out this online form: https://example.com/form

Spaces are limited, so please RSVP as soon as possible. I look forward to seeing you at the seminar.

Sincerely,

Your name

For me, this needs a little more work/detail, but it's a great start. Nevertheless I tried again and ChatGPT came up with this as an alternative:

Subject: Invitation: Master Your Future at Our Free Retirement Planning Seminar

Dear [Recipient's Name],

We trust this message finds you well.

We would like to extend an exclusive invitation to join us at Denbies Vineyard in Dorking for a unique afternoon of learning and networking, as part of our upcoming seminar - "Pathways to Prosperity: Navigating the Road to Retirement."

This seminar is especially designed for pre-retirement business owners in Guildford and the wider Surrey area. It is set for Saturday, 27th May, beginning at 2pm and running for approximately two hours.

As a business owner, preparing for retirement can present its own unique set of challenges and opportunities. This seminar aims to equip you with the knowledge and tools needed to confidently plan for your financial future. You will gain insight into the best strategies to optimise your retirement plan, learn about diversifying income streams, managing risks, tax implications, and much more.

Here are several benefits of attending:

- Expert Guidance: Our experienced financial planners will share valuable insights on creating a comprehensive and flexible retirement plan.
- Networking Opportunities: You will have the chance to connect and engage with other local business owners, fostering a stronger business community and potentially leading to meaningful partnerships and collaborations.
- A Scenic Venue: Enjoy the beautiful setting of Denbies Vineyard, the UK's largest vineyard, which provides a relaxing and inspiring backdrop for the seminar.
- Wine Tasting: To conclude the event in style, we invite you to join us for a

complimentary wine tasting session, sampling some of Denbies' finest offerings.

To RSVP, kindly choose from the following options:

- Email: Please send us an email at [your email address], indicating your name and the number of attendees.
- Phone: Call us directly at [your contact number] and provide your details.
- Online: Visit our website at [your website URL] and fill out the RSVP form under the event details.

We would be delighted to see you at the seminar. Your presence would undoubtedly contribute to the richness of our discussions. If you have any questions or require further information, please do not hesitate to reach out to us.

We look forward to helping you pave your pathway to a prosperous retirement!

Warm regards,

[Your Name]

[Your Title]

[Your Company]

[Your Contact Information]

Again, it's still not quite there but very much on the right track. One trick is to ask the AI to put itself in the shoes of the attendee/persona and to then write the invitation in a way that will specifically appeal to them.

Summary

So hopefully you can see that from our list of essential marketing materials, we can get even the most complex of tasks completed in a matter of seconds. In fact writing the prompt takes up most of the time...

My advice is to revisit your 'marketing things-to-do' list - and start getting them done.

Your Notes

Prompt Engineering

Where the Magic Happens

Finally on the subject of skills, we should spend a bit more time on how we go about getting the best results from Generative AI. It's commonly known as **Prompt Engineering**.

As we saw in the previous chapter, in the early stage of an adviser's journey into AI adoption, they will usually find that the technology can be used highly effectively for marketing and client communications. So let's expand further on this.

For well over forty years I've been helping IFAs and advisers with ideas and strategies to attract new leads, prospects and clients. My book *Marketing and Lead Generation for Financial Advice Professionals* has almost five hundred pages of ideas that different advisers can use. That said, and with the best will in the world, whilst there is an eagerness to try out various marketing tactics, a great many advisers simply don't have the time, wherewithal, skills or budget to actually get it done.

So with the arrival of AI, their problems are solved at a stroke.

But, and it's a big 'but', as the old saying goes *"Garbage in, garbage out"*.

Although tools like ChatGPT can make a reasonably good job of creating marketing content even with poor prompting [telling the software what you want it to do], your results can be transformed with well-crafted and thoroughly thought through instructions (prompts).

Prompt Engineering is a process used in working with AI language models, like ChatGPT from OpenAI. It involves carefully crafting and structuring the input prompts to these models to guide and optimise the responses they generate.

For a financial planner using an AI assistant, this could mean figuring out how to phrase your questions or statements to the AI to get the most useful and relevant financial advice or information.

For instance, instead of asking:

"What's the best investment?"

…which is vague, you might ask:

"What are some suitable investment options for a 45-year-old client with moderate risk tolerance and a diversified portfolio?"

This is a more specific prompt that will guide the AI in generating a more targeted, beneficial response.

It's like learning the best way to ask a question or pose a problem to get the response you need, enhancing the effectiveness of the AI tool in your financial planning practice.

Prompt Engineering doesn't require programming skills but rather, a good understanding of your AI tool's capabilities and your desired outcome. It's a trial-and-error process, refining the way you interact with the AI to improve its utility in your work.

Let's use the analogy of a navigation system:

Imagine you're using a GPS to navigate your way to a destination. The way you input your destination into the GPS can greatly affect the quality of the directions you receive.

If you're vague and just type in "restaurant," the GPS might lead you to the nearest fast-food joint when what you actually wanted was a high-end Italian restaurant. In this case, the prompt "restaurant" was far too broad for the GPS to understand your actual need.

Now, consider instead if you typed in "Italian restaurant with good reviews in London." This prompt is more detailed and will give the GPS a better understanding of what you're looking for, resulting in directions to a location that's a better fit for your evening out.

Prompt Engineering is similar to this process. Just like with the GPS or maps tool, the way you phrase your requests to an AI can greatly impact the quality of the response.

Being more specific and clear with your prompts can help guide the AI to provide more useful and accurate information for your needs.

Example Prompts

Here are 30 examples of how a financial planner can optimise their prompts when using an AI tool to generate marketing materials:

Poor: "Write a blog post."

Good: "Write a blog post about the 5 most common mistakes people make when planning for retirement."

Poor: "Create a social media post."

Good: "Create a social media post promoting our new financial advisory services for young professionals in the tech industry."

Poor: "Draft an article."

Good: "Draft an article explaining the impact of the recent tax law changes on small business owners."

Poor: "Press release."

Good: "Write a press release announcing our financial advice firm's recent certification in ISO22222 The Financial Planner Standard of Excellence, and what this means to clients."

Poor: "LinkedIn post about our services."

Good: "Create a LinkedIn post highlighting the benefits of our comprehensive wealth management services for recent retirees."

Poor: "Email to clients."

Good: "Draft an email to our clients providing an update on the recent volatility in the stock market and our recommended course of action."

Poor: "Financial tips blog post."

Good: "Write a blog post sharing 7 tips for saving for a child's university education."

Poor: "Article about investments."

Good: "Write an informative and lengthy article explaining the pros and cons of ESG investing.

Poor: "Marketing post for Facebook."

Good: "Create an engaging Facebook post to promote our upcoming webinar on estate planning."

Poor: "Estate planning guide."

Good: "Create a comprehensive guide for beginners on the key steps involved in estate planning. Make the guide comprehensive but add some humour as it can be a 'dry' topic for some."

Poor: "Newsletter content."

Good: "Create content for our monthly newsletter, highlighting the recent changes in interest rates and their impact on mortgage loans."

Poor: "Article on finance tips."

Good: "Write an article providing 10 finance tips for self-employed individuals in the Leeds area. Then expand on each of these tips and write me a script I can use when making a YouTube video on the topic."

Poor: “Write a blog about the benefits of equity release and later life lending for people living in Manchester.”

Good: “Write an in-depth but engaging article on the pros and cons of equity release plans for homeowners over the age of 55 in Manchester. Highlight common myths around equity release and include examples.”

Poor: "Retirement planning blog post."

Good: "Write a blog post explaining different ways that people can save for retirement. Include simple examples and some more complex ones which maximise tax opportunities."

Poor: "Write about our new service."

Good: "Create a detailed announcement for our website about our new tax planning service for freelancers. Create another version which is in the form of a press release."

Poor: "Social media post about finance."

Good: "Create a series of Instagram posts sharing daily budgeting tips for millennials. Make them humorous and fun."

Poor: "Email about market changes."

Good: "Draft a reassuring email to our clients about the current bear market and our strategies for managing their portfolios."

Poor: "Post about our financial seminar."

Good: "Write a compelling LinkedIn post inviting small business owners in London to our upcoming seminar on financial risk management. Include ten bullet points covering the benefits of joining the webinar."

Poor: "Article about wealth management."

Good: "Write an article demystifying the process of wealth management for new entrepreneurs. Include a powerful analogy which helps people to better understand the process."

Poor: "Blog post about financial planning."

Good: "Write a blog post about the importance of having a diversified portfolio in long-term financial planning. Give examples as to why diversification is important."

Poor: "Press release about company award."

Good: "Write a press release about our financial planning firm winning the 'Best Customer Service' award in our city. Include how this will benefit our clients."

Poor: "Marketing email."

Good: "Create a compelling marketing email promoting our upcoming free consultation sessions for new clients. Explain that we typically work with self-employed individuals."

Poor: "Post about financial advice."

Good: "Create a Twitter thread which demystifies the role of a financial adviser for recent university graduates. Include examples of why starting early in life can be highly beneficial."

Poor: "Guide for clients."

Good: "Create a step-by-step guide to understanding and interpreting financial statements for our small business owner clients."

Poor: "Blog post about investing."

Good: "Write a beginner-friendly blog post explaining the concept of compound interest and its importance in investing. Include examples."

Poor: "Post about tax season."

Good: "Craft an informative Instagram carousel post providing tips for stress-free tax preparation."

Poor: "Email about client meeting."

Good: "Draft a professional email inviting our clients to a webinar discussing market trends and our outlook for the next quarter."

Poor: "Article about financial trends."

Good: "Write an article analysing the emerging trends in sustainable investing and what they mean for our clients."

Poor: "Post about financial adviser role."

Good: "Create a LinkedIn article explaining what a financial adviser does and how working with one can benefit individuals at different stages of their life. Include examples from different life stages."

Poor: "Article about financial planning"

Good: "Write an engaging article of five thousand words explaining what financial planning is and how it works. Make reference to lifestyle financial planning and include examples."

Poor: "Content for financial seminar."

Good: "Create engaging presentation content for our upcoming seminar on 'Navigating Personal Finance during a Pandemic'."

Poor: "Letter to local accountants."

Good: "Create a professional but friendly letter that I can send to firms of accountants in our area. Introduce ourselves, explain what we do and how having a relationship with us can potentially be mutually beneficial."

More advanced examples:

Poor: "Personalised article for dentists."

Good: "Write a personalised article outlining investment strategies specifically tailored for dentists nearing retirement."

Even better: "Write a personalised article outlining investment strategies specifically tailored for female dentists nearing retirement. Take into account the unique career path of dentists in private practice."

Highly detailed: "Please write a personalised article tailored specifically for accomplished female dentists who are nearing retirement. This article should provide valuable insights, advice and considerations to support them in this unique phase of their lives.

Explore the journey of female dentists who are approaching retirement in detail. The article should recognise their dedication, celebrate their accomplishments and address the challenges they may face during this transition.

Sections to Include:

Reflecting on a Fulfilling Career: Highlight the achievements and milestones of female dentists, emphasising the positive impact they have made on their patients' lives.

Preparing for Retirement: Discuss financial considerations, creating an exit strategy and managing the transition period effectively.

Nurturing Personal Well-being: Address the importance of self-care, exploring new interests and building a support network for a fulfilling retirement.

Embracing the Next Chapter: Inspire female dentists to reinvent their identity, leave a lasting legacy and prioritise health and wellness.

Conclusion: Wrap up the article by emphasising the significance of female dentists' contributions, providing encouragement and empowering them to embrace the next chapter of their lives with excitement and confidence.

Please make the article informative and engaging, and use a warm and supportive tone throughout."

Poor: "Welcome letter to new clients"

Very good: "I am a financial planner in Bristol in the UK, and I would like you [ChatGPT] to help me create a welcome letter for new clients. The letter should convey our excitement in welcoming them, emphasise our commitment to providing excellent service and encourage open communication.

Additionally, please include a section encouraging clients to refer us to their friends and family if they find our services valuable. The letter should be warm, inviting and showcase our dedication to helping clients achieve their financial goals. Please provide the letter in a friendly but professional and engaging tone."

You can see from that last two prompts that they are pretty detailed. Don't be afraid to be thorough in your prompts because it will make the results you get much more useful.

And if you are wondering, the following is what ChatGPT produced when I gave it that exact prompt just now:

Subject: Welcome to [Your Financial Planning Firm's Name] - Let's Begin Your Financial Journey!

Dear [Client's Name],

We are thrilled to extend a warm welcome to you as our newest client at [Your Financial Planning Firm's Name]. As a dedicated financial planner in Bristol, UK, we are excited to embark on this journey with you and assist you in achieving your financial goals.

In this welcome letter, we want to express our genuine enthusiasm in having you as part of our client community. We believe in building strong and lasting relationships, and we are committed to providing you with exceptional service every step of the way.

At [Your Financial Planning Firm's Name], we understand that financial planning is a personal and important aspect of your life. That is why we are here to guide and support you, ensuring that your financial aspirations become a reality. We take pride in offering a comprehensive range of services, tailored to your unique needs, including retirement planning, investment strategies, tax optimisation, estate planning, and more.

Our commitment to you goes beyond the services we offer. We firmly believe that open and transparent communication is the foundation of a successful financial partnership. We encourage you to reach out to us with any questions, concerns, or updates regarding your financial situation. Whether it's a phone call, an email, or an in-person meeting, our team is here to listen, provide guidance, and offer solutions. Your financial journey is personal, and we are dedicated to supporting you throughout this process.

In addition, we would like to express our gratitude for choosing [Your Financial Planning Firm's Name].

We understand that trust is earned, and we are honoured that you have entrusted us with your financial well-being. We are committed to working diligently on your behalf, ensuring that your goals remain our top priority. Your success is our success.

We kindly request that if you find value in our services, and you believe that your friends, family, or colleagues could benefit from our expertise, please consider introducing us to them. By sharing your positive experience, you can help us extend our reach and assist more individuals in achieving financial stability and prosperity. Rest assured that anyone you refer to us will receive the same level of care and dedication that you have come to expect from us.

Once again, welcome to [Your Financial Planning Firm's Name]. We are excited to have you on board and look forward to helping you navigate the intricacies of financial planning. If you have any questions or require assistance, please don't hesitate to reach out. Together, we will create a roadmap to achieve your financial goals and secure a prosperous future.

Warm regards,

[Your Name]
[Your Position]

[Your Financial Planning Firm's Name]
[Contact Information]

Add Icing to the Cake

Now, you may well be thinking that the letter you have just read is too long, too formal, too informal, too 'OTT', too whatever. And you would be right - every adviser will have their own view on what a good welcome letter should look like.

The point is that the AI has done the leg work and it's now down to you to fine tune it to your particular tone, style and way of speaking. In fact I deliberately 'over cooked' this prompt/letter to show you what is possible, and it would now be down to you to tweak it to your requirements. You'll discover that the more you use ChatGPT and other generative AI tools, the more you will adapt to its capabilities and your prompts will become more and more accurate.

Akin to a beautifully baked cake that still needs that final flourish of icing to truly shine, ChatGPT's output often requires a layer of personalisation to resonate with your particular audience. This is where your expertise as financial planners and advisers comes into play. As experts in the field, you understand the specific needs, tonality and style that your content needs to embody. So consider ChatGPT as a **collaborator** in your content creation process.

This collaboration between ChatGPT and your financial expertise ensures an efficient content creation process. It allows you to maintain a consistent and high-quality content flow, saving you time, and allowing you to focus more on strategic tasks.

Remember, while ChatGPT can bake an excellent content 'cake', your skills and insights are the 'icing' that transforms it into an irresistible treat for your audience. The more specific and clear you are with your prompts, the better the AI tool can understand your needs and produce the content you need.

Towards the end of this book you will find over one hundred and forty specimen prompts that you can use with ChatGPT and other AI tools. Play around with them, tweak them to your own business and then use them!

Your Notes

Roadmap Summary

Your Pathway to AI Success Unveiled

The financial advisory industry is experiencing a transformative shift, propelled by the advent of AI. As professionals within the profession and wider industry, it is crucial that we understand, accept and strategically leverage this technology to enhance our businesses.

This is not an option – it's an essential move towards future-proofing our practices. This report provided an elaborate roadmap for seamlessly integrating AI into financial advisory practices, complete with a timeline and strategic milestones.

The journey commences with the appointment of an AI Champion and unfolds through eight distinct, purposeful stages:

1. Recognising the need and appointing your AI Champion
2. Awareness and Education
3. Exploration and Identification
4. Planning and Prioritising
5. Pilot Testing
6. Evaluation and Adjustment

7. Rollout and Expansion, and
8. Continuous Learning and Updating.

In addition, key pillars of change management were underlined as essential elements to support the successful integration of AI. These are:

- Clear communication
- Robust training
- Leadership involvement
- Incremental implementation
- Employee engagement
- Celebration of progress, and
- Embracing the spirit of continuous improvement.

Central to navigating this transformative process is the adoption of a proactive approach. By proactively understanding and integrating AI into our businesses, we are not just reacting to changes in the industry but taking the lead in driving these changes. This enables us to stay ahead of industry trends, enhance our service offerings and improve our operational efficiencies. A proactive approach empowers us to shape our services according to the evolving demands of our clients, thereby ensuring we remain relevant and competitive.

Moreover, being proactive allows us to mitigate potential challenges associated with AI adoption by addressing them early in the process. It also lets us maximise the benefits of AI by aligning its capabilities with our strategic goals right from the outset.

The proactive integration of AI is, therefore, not a matter of choice but a strategic imperative for ensuring the continued delivery of superior services to our clients.

Let this book be your guide towards a future where AI is seen not as a looming threat, but as a potent tool, capable of taking our financial advisory practices to new heights of efficiency and excellence.

Your Notes

Quick Wins: Leveraging AI for Immediate Impact

Stop Playing with AI – Use It!

In today's fast-paced and digitally driven business landscape, embracing AI will undoubtedly become a strategic imperative for financial planning firms. While a comprehensive AI adoption strategy requires careful planning and implementation, it's essential to recognise that there are quick wins that can provide immediate benefits and strengthen your confidence in wider AI adoption.

By leveraging tools like ChatGPT, financial planning firms can tap into the power of AI to achieve quick wins that deliver tangible results. These quick wins typically focus on areas such as:

- Marketing
- Content creation
- Client engagement
- Automation
- Personalisation. and
- Efficiency.

They allow firms to experience the immediate impact of AI while laying the foundation for broader AI integration in the future.

One area where AI can make an immediate difference is in content creation. By harnessing the capabilities of ChatGPT, financial planning firms can generate high-quality and engaging content for marketing efforts, including blog posts, articles, social media captions and personalised client communications. This helps establish thought leadership, attract new clients and deliver tailored messages that resonate with specific target audiences.

Additionally, AI-powered chatbots can revolutionise customer support by providing real-time assistance, answering frequently asked questions and guiding website visitors through the initial stages of engagement. This not only enhances the customer experience but also frees up valuable time for financial planners to focus on more complex client needs.

Lead generation and qualification can also be optimised through AI. By leveraging interactive tools like quizzes/scorecards or calculators powered by ChatGPT, firms can engage potential clients, capture valuable data and qualify leads more effectively. These tools provide personalised insights and recommendations, establishing a strong foundation for meaningful client interactions.

Furthermore, AI can enhance market research and competitive analysis by analysing large volumes of data and extracting valuable insights. It helps firms stay informed about industry trends, client sentiment and emerging opportunities, enabling data-driven decision-making and a competitive edge.

In this section, we explore these quick wins and highlight the areas where ChatGPT, as an AI tool, can make an immediate difference. We delve into specific use cases, ranging from personalised content creation and targeted marketing campaigns to client engagement, automation and continuous learning.

By leveraging these quick wins, financial planning firms can unlock the immediate benefits of AI adoption while building a solid foundation for further AI integration and transformation.

Content Creation Ideas:

- Blog posts, articles and social media captions.
- Personalised client communications, reports and newsletters.
- Customised financial education materials.
- Customer Support and Chatbots:

Chat Support System for Website Visitors:

- Virtual financial assistant for on-demand guidance.
- Chatbots trained on your own data.
- Automated meeting minutes and support.

Lead Generation and Qualification:

- Interactive lead generation tools, quizzes or calculators.
- Personalised outputs based on data entered into online assessments.
- Personalised email marketing campaigns for targeted engagement.

Market Research and Competitive Analysis:

- Analysing market trends and conducting competitive analysis.
- Social listening and sentiment analysis for insights.
- Monitoring competitors' website content and learning best practices.

Personalisation and Customisation:

- Dynamic investment reports tailored to individual portfolios.
- Personalised retirement planning reports and tax planning guides.
- Tailored client presentations and onboarding materials.

Automation and Efficiency:

- Automated data analysis for insights and decision-making.
- Automated risk assessment and risk tolerance questionnaires.
- Automated report generation for efficiency and consistency.

Marketing and Advertising:

- Targeted content marketing campaigns for specific niches.
- Targeted social media advertising for audience engagement.
- Creation of targeted graphics for niche markets

Financial Tools and Calculators:

- Interactive financial planning tools for scenario analysis.
- Customised calculators for investment projections and analysis.

Client Engagement and Personalised Experiences:

- Highly personalised content generation for individual clients or niche groups.
- Personalised financial education resources and materials.
- Presentation skills feedback from online meetings

Continuous Learning and Improvement:

- Staying updated with the latest AI advancements.
- Fostering a culture of continuous learning and innovation.
- Encouraging advisers to proactively explore new AI applications.

For more applications, join our dedicated AI Best Practice Group for financial advisers at https://ai-best-practice-for-advisers.scoreapp.com

By leveraging these quick wins, your financial planning firm can experience immediate benefits in marketing, content generation, client engagement, automation, personalisation and efficiency. These wins can serve as catalysts for wider AI adoption, strengthening your confidence in AI's potential to transform your business.

Your Notes

Arrival on the Opposite Riverbank

The Story Continues

As financial advisers crossed the metaphorical river and embraced AI in their businesses, a new world unfolded before them. In this new world, AI became an integral part of their daily operations, transforming the way they interacted with clients, analysed data and delivered financial advice. Let's explore this transformed world and also consider the fate of those who did not cross the river.

For those financial advisers who embraced AI, they found themselves equipped with powerful tools that enhanced their capabilities. AI-driven chatbots became their reliable virtual assistants, handling routine inquiries and providing quick responses, allowing advisers to focus on more complex client needs.

Personalised client communications were automated, allowing for tailored reports, newsletters and educational materials that resonated with individual clients' goals and preferences. AI-powered data analysis provided valuable insights, enabling more accurate risk assessments, portfolio optimisation and data-driven decision-making. In this new world, financial advisers thrived by leveraging AI to deliver personalised, efficient and impactful financial planning services.

However, it's important to acknowledge that not all financial advisers were able to cross the river and embrace AI. Some remained on the other side, hesitant to adapt and change. Their reasons for staying behind varied: fear of the unknown, resistance to technology, or a belief that the traditional ways of doing business would still suffice. Unfortunately, their hesitation limited their ability to keep up with the evolving industry landscape.

Over time, the divide between those who embraced AI and those who did not grew wider. Financial advisers who crossed the river and embraced AI experienced significant growth in their client base, expanded service offerings and improved operational efficiency. They were better equipped to navigate the complexities of the digital era and address the evolving needs of clients in an increasingly data-driven world.

On the other hand, those who remained on the other side found themselves struggling to keep up. They faced increasing competition from firms that leveraged AI to provide personalised and efficient services. Without the benefits of AI-driven automation and data insights, their ability to deliver tailored advice and meet client expectations diminished. Over time, many of these advisers faced dwindling client numbers and struggled to compete in the rapidly evolving financial planning landscape.

~

The story of the river serves as a reminder that embracing AI is **not just an option but a necessity** for financial advisers in today's digital age.

The world they find themselves in after crossing the river is one of opportunities, growth and innovation. By harnessing the power of AI, financial advisers can provide personalised, efficient and value-driven services that meet the evolving needs of their clients.

The fate of those who did not cross the river serves as a cautionary tale, highlighting the importance of adaptability, embracing change and continuously evolving to stay relevant in a rapidly transforming industry.

The Power of Personalisation

The Pathway to Tailored Financial Advice Services

Hopefully it won't have escaped your notice that I have referred to personalisation on several occasions throughout this book.

And that's important, because personalisation is one of the most crucial distinguishing factors in today's competitive financial landscape.

Utilising AI for personalisation in a financial planning business not only gives it a competitive edge but also increases client satisfaction and retention. The transformative potential of AI in personalising various facets of the service, from marketing strategies to client communications, cannot be overstated.

For financial planners and Independent Financial Advisers (IFAs), the core service revolves around understanding a client's financial goals, current status and the level of risk they are willing to assume. Traditionally, this required extensive client interaction and manual data analysis. With AI, however, this process can be streamlined and significantly optimised. AI systems can leverage vast amounts of data to offer personalised financial advice based on the client's unique situation, risk profile and objectives. This level of personalisation enables planners and advisers to offer precise, tailored advice that resonates more with the client and instils trust in the financial relationship.

AI-driven personalisation extends to marketing strategies as well. By understanding a client's preferences, behaviours and needs, AI can tailor marketing content to target specific client niches more effectively. This personalisation goes beyond basic demographic details to encompass behaviour, past interactions, and client sentiments. This level of granular targeting facilitates highly relevant, personalised communications that resonate with the client, increasing engagement rates and ultimately the likelihood of client conversion, retention and referrals.

What's more, using AI, IFAs and financial planners can automate and personalise routine communications, saving valuable time while enhancing the client experience. Whether it's transaction confirmations, portfolio updates, or financial market news, AI can tailor these messages to the client's preferences, making them feel seen, understood and even more highly valued.

Failure to integrate AI into a financial planning business could lead to a lack of personalisation, which is increasingly becoming a significant expectation from clients. Businesses that don't capitalise on the benefits of AI risk falling behind in a rapidly evolving marketplace, where client-centric, personalised experiences are the new norm.

In conclusion, personalisation is an imperative in a modern financial planning business, both for offering customised services and for effectively connecting with and retaining clients. AI stands as a pivotal tool in achieving this personalisation, driving client satisfaction and business growth alike.

Here are just a few ways that advisers and financial planners could personalise communications with individual clients and niche groups:

Personalised Financial Reports:

Tailoring financial reports to the needs and interests of each client or client group, highlighting specific areas of their portfolio or aspects of the market that they care about most.

Customised Notifications and Alerts:

Providing notifications on market changes, portfolio performance, or financial news that's relevant to individual clients or groups based on their portfolio and personal interests.

Tailored Educational Content:

Sending learning materials (like articles, eBooks or videos) relevant to the financial products, strategies or market trends that the client or client group is interested in or has recently enquired about.

Personalised Reminders:

Sending custom reminders for key dates like investment maturity dates, tax filing deadlines, or scheduled financial reviews that are specific to the client or group.

Custom Client Portals:

Creating client portals that are personalised for each client, providing information, reports, and updates that are tailored to their specific interests, portfolio and financial objectives.

Individualised Marketing Campaigns:

Tailoring marketing messages to reflect the needs, interests and aspirations of specific clients or client groups. This could involve promoting relevant products or services, or highlighting case studies and success stories that would resonate with them.

Segmented Email Communication:

Designing email communications that address the specific needs or queries of individual clients or groups. This could include different tips, advice or insights for clients at different stages of their financial journey or with different investment goals.

Personalised Service Proposals:

Crafting personalised proposals that highlight the particular benefits a specific service or product can provide to a client or client group based on their financial goals, risk profile and life situation.

Tailored Video Messages:

Using AI tools to create personalised video messages for special occasions, reminders, or important financial updates, adding a more personal and engaging touch to the communication.

Chatbots and Virtual Assistants:

Using AI-powered chatbots or virtual assistants to answer client queries in real-time and provide personalised financial advice or information. This not only improves the customer experience but also frees up valuable time for the financial planner.

With a mind to considering Consumer Duty obligations, it's worth expanding on the use of AI to tailor and personalise educational content.

The use of tailored educational content plays a pivotal role in building meaningful and long-lasting relationships with clients. Clients appreciate not just service, but also guidance and knowledge to make informed financial decisions. This is where the role of AI becomes profoundly impactful for financial planners.

AI systems are capable of processing vast amounts of data, including a client's financial history, preferences, interactions and even their behavioural patterns. With this data, (with advisers being mindful of data protection and privacy), AI can determine the type of educational content that would be most beneficial to a client or a specific group of clients. It can help financial planners identify the most appropriate topics, ranging from retirement planning strategies and investment trends to tax-saving tips and market analysis. This degree of personalisation helps engage clients by providing them with useful insights tailored to their specific needs and interests.

Furthermore, AI can not only identify suitable topics, but it can also recommend the most effective format for delivering the content. Some clients may prefer reading in-depth articles, while others may find infographics or short video explainers more engaging. AI can analyse a client's past engagement with different content types and use this data to customise the format of future educational materials.

Besides individual client communication, AI can also identify niche groups among a financial planner's clientele. These groups might share common traits or preferences, such as being retirees, first-time investors, high net-worth individuals, or perhaps those interested in sustainable investing. AI can help create customised educational content for these specific groups, further enhancing the relevance and value of the content.

In addition, AI's capabilities are not limited to the creation of personalised educational content.

It can also optimise its delivery. For example, AI can determine the best time to send an email or a notification based on the client's previous engagement patterns, increasing the likelihood of the content being consumed.

In summary, by providing personalised educational content, financial planners can demonstrate their commitment to helping clients improve their financial literacy and make informed decisions and therefore help achieve good outcomes. AI's data processing and pattern recognition capabilities are instrumental in creating and delivering such content, making it a powerful tool for enhancing client engagement and satisfaction.

Your Notes

Bullet Point Summary and Next Steps for Financial Advisers

In-depth and Quick Start Versions

In-depth summary:

Self-Assessment and Goal Setting:

- Reflect on key insights and evaluate your business readiness for AI adoption.
- Identify specific areas where AI can bring significant benefits and set goals.
- Consider client communication, automation, data analysis and personalisation.
- Determine measurable objectives and timelines to track progress.
- Align goals with business objectives and client needs.

AI Opportunity Mapping:

- Create a visual map of your financial advisory processes.

- Identify pain points, inefficiencies and opportunities for improvement.
- Brainstorm AI-powered solutions and tools to enhance identified processes.
- Prioritise opportunities based on impact and feasibility.
- Consider scalability and integration capabilities of potential solutions.

Client Persona and Personalised AI Experience:

- Develop client personas based on target audience segments.
- Analyse unique needs, preferences and pain points for each segment.
- Explore ways to leverage AI for personalised experiences and services.
- Define strategies for tailored communications, recommendations and interactions.
- Enhance client satisfaction and engagement through personalised AI solutions.

Technology Assessment and Vendor Research:

- Evaluate existing technology infrastructure and identify gaps for AI integration.
- Research AI vendors and solutions that align with your business goals.
- Consider capabilities, reputation, customer reviews and integration compatibility.
- Create a shortlist of potential partners for further evaluation and engagement.
- Choose vendors that offer scalable, secure and customisable AI solutions.

Change Management and Implementation Plan:

- Craft a comprehensive change management plan for AI adoption.
- Address organisational and cultural aspects, communication and training needs.
- Define an implementation roadmap with milestones, timelines and resource allocation.
- Involve key stakeholders and communicate the benefits of AI adoption.
- Ensure alignment with the overall business strategy and client expectations.

Develop an AI Implementation Strategy:

- Define clear action steps, timelines and resource allocation.
- Align the strategy with business objectives and client needs.
- Identify specific AI opportunities for implementation.

Collaborate with AI Experts and Peers:

- Seek guidance from industry experts and peers.
- Join the LifeTalk AI Best Practice Group at https://ai-best-practice-for-advisers.scoreapp.com

- Engage in knowledge-sharing platforms and communities.
- Attend conferences, webinars and training programs on AI adoption.

Pilot Test AI Solutions:

- Select one or two AI opportunities for pilot testing.
- Evaluate performance, effectiveness and user experience.

- Collect feedback and refine implementation approach.

Iterate, Learn and Scale:

- Iterate and refine AI adoption approach based on outcomes.
- Learn from successes and challenges encountered during the pilot phase.
- Scale up AI implementation across other identified areas.

Continual Learning and Adaptation:

- Stay updated on the latest AI advancements and industry trends.
- Foster a culture of innovation and continuous learning.
- Assess new AI opportunities to enhance financial advisory services.

By following these steps, financial advisers can take actionable measures to integrate AI into their businesses, driving growth, efficiency and client satisfaction.

Quick-Start Summary

First:

Identify Quick Win Areas:

Assess your financial advisory practice and identify areas where AI can provide quick wins and immediate benefits. Focus on tasks or processes that can be easily automated, streamlined, or enhanced through AI technology.

Prioritise Opportunities:

Evaluate the potential impact and feasibility of each quick win opportunity. Prioritise them based on their potential to improve efficiency, enhance client experience, or generate cost savings. Consider the readiness of your current technology infrastructure and the level of effort required for implementation.

Research AI Solutions:

Conduct focused research on AI solutions that align with your identified quick win areas. Look for off-the-shelf AI tools or platforms that are specifically designed for financial advisory purposes. Consider factors such as ease of implementation, user-friendliness, scalability and compatibility with your existing systems.

Evaluate Vendor Options:

Shortlist a few AI solution providers that seem promising based on your research. Request demos or trials of their products to assess their functionality, features and usability. Consider factors such as customer support, reputation and pricing structure to make an informed decision.

Next Steps:

Plan Implementation:

Create a high-level implementation plan for integrating AI into your quick win areas. Define key milestones, timelines and resource allocation. Consider any necessary changes to workflows or processes to accommodate the AI solutions.

Collaborate with AI Experts:

Seek advice or consultation from AI experts who specialise in the financial advisory domain. Engage in brief consultations or workshops to gain insights into best practices, implementation strategies and potential challenges to anticipate.

Pilot Test AI Solutions:

Select one or two AI solutions from your quick win areas and initiate pilot testing. Implement the chosen solutions in a controlled environment, monitoring their performance, effectiveness and user experience. Gather feedback from advisers and clients to refine the implementation approach and address any issues.

Iterate and Scale:

Based on the results of the pilot phase, iterate and refine your AI implementation approach. Make necessary adjustments to optimise the solutions and expand their usage to additional areas. Gradually scale up the adoption of AI across your financial advisory practice.

Continuous Learning:

Stay updated on the latest AI advancements and industry trends. Continually explore new AI opportunities that can further enhance your practice. Engage in ongoing learning, attend webinars or workshops and collaborate with industry peers to share insights and experiences.

By following this Quick Start approach and the subsequent steps, financial advisers can kickstart their AI adoption journey, realising immediate benefits while laying the foundation for broader integration in the future.

Your Notes

Bonus Section:

140 Prompts Financial Advisers Can Use with ChatGPT and Other Generative AI Tools to Create Compelling Marketing Content

Unleashing the Magic

Use these prompts as the starting point for creating content for your website, Twitter, blogs, videos, LinkedIn etc. Then manually add your own 'spin', tone and style to tweak the results or make them more natural.

AI can do this too with prompts such as "Make this less formal" or "Add some humour" or "Make this more serious", "Expand on XYZ point" etc.

Remember - the AI (ChatGPT) bakes the cake – then you add the icing.

Good luck and have fun with these!

1. Write five bullet points on the benefits of having a financial plan

2. Write a short article on how to set financial goals

3. Write three tweets about the importance of saving for retirement

4. Write a short blog post about the impact of inflation on investments

5. Write a bullet-pointed list of the key considerations when choosing a financial adviser

6. Write a short article on the difference between different risk tolerances

7. Write three tweets about the benefits of diversification in investing

8. Write a short blog post on the impact of taxes on investments and how to minimise them

9. Write a bullet-pointed list of the different types of insurance and their importance in a financial plan

10. Write a short article on the importance of estate planning

11. Write three tweets about the importance of starting to save for college early

12. Write a short blog post about the risks and rewards of real estate investment

13. Write a bullet-pointed list of the key factors to consider when creating a budget

14. Write a short article on the importance of managing debt

15. Write three tweets about the benefits of financial planning during a career transition

16. Write a short blog post about the benefits of annuities in retirement planning

17. Write a bullet-pointed list of the key considerations for risk management in a financial plan

18. Write a short article for posting on LinkedIn on the importance of planning for long-term care expenses

19. Write three tweets about the benefits of reviewing and updating your financial plan

regularly

20. Write a short blog post on the benefits of having a financial plan for stress-free financial decision making
21. Write a short article on the importance of emergency savings in financial planning
22. Write three tweets about the benefits of regularly monitoring your investments
23. Write a short blog post on the role of life insurance in a comprehensive financial plan
24. Write a bullet-pointed list of the benefits of working with a financial planner
25. Write a short article on the importance of setting realistic financial goals
26. Write three tweets about the impact of market volatility on investments and how to handle it
27. Write a short blog post on the difference between saving and investing
28. Write a bullet-pointed list of the key considerations for investing in stocks

29. Write a short article on the importance of saving for unexpected expenses

30. Write three tweets about the benefits of a diversified portfolio

31. Write a short blog post on the pros and cons of different investment options

32. Write a bullet-pointed list of the key considerations for investing in bonds

33. Write a short article on the importance of having a well-rounded investment strategy

34. Write three tweets about the benefits of financial planning for small business owners

35. Write a short blog post on the impact of market changes on investments and how to respond

36. Write a bullet-pointed list of the key considerations for investing in real estate

37. Write a short article on the benefits of financial planning for families with multiple financial goals

38. Write three tweets about the importance of having a plan for managing debt

39. Write a short blog post on the benefits of having a long-term investment strategy

40. Write a bullet-pointed list of the key considerations for retirement planning

41. Write three tweets about the basics of financial planning for beginners

42. Write a short blog post on the importance of creating a budget in financial planning

43. Write the text for a video on the steps to creating a financial plan

44. Write a bullet-pointed list of the most common financial planning mistakes and how to avoid them

45. Write a short article on the importance of saving for retirement in your 20s and 30s

46. Write three tweets about the benefits of seeking professional financial advice

47. Write a short blog post on the impact of inflation on your financial plan and how to

counteract it

48. Write the text for a video on the best ways to manage debt

49. Write a bullet-pointed list of the key elements of a comprehensive financial plan

50. Write a short article on the importance of understanding investment risks and returns

51. Write three tweets about the benefits of creating a financial plan for a secure future

52. Write a short blog post on the impact of life events on financial planning and how to prepare for them

53. Write the text for a video on the benefits of setting financial goals and how to achieve them

54. Write a bullet-pointed list of the most effective ways to save money in a financial plan

55. Write a short article on the importance of understanding the role of taxes in financial planning

56. Write three tweets about the benefits of considering all financial aspects when making big purchases

57. Write a short blog post on the impact of financial planning on mental and emotional wellbeing

58. Write the text for a video on the best ways to save for college expenses in a financial plan

59. Write a bullet-pointed list of the most common financial planning myths and why they're not true

60. Write a short article on the importance of regularly reviewing and updating your financial plan

61. Write three tweets about the importance of diversification in investment portfolios

62. Write a short blog post on the benefits of automating your finances through a financial planning app

63. Write the text for a video on the steps to creating an emergency fund

64. Write a bullet-pointed list of the most effective ways to reduce monthly expenses

in a financial plan

65. Write a short article on the impact of credit score on your financial plan and how to improve it

66. Write three tweets about the benefits of having a long-term investment strategy

67. Write a short blog post on the importance of knowing your risk tolerance in investment planning

68. Write the text for a video on the best ways to save for a down payment on a home

69. Write a bullet-pointed list of the key considerations for choosing the right financial adviser

70. Write a short article on the importance of estate planning in a comprehensive financial plan

71. Write three tweets about the benefits of using technology in financial planning

72. Write a short blog post on the impact of interest rates on investment portfolios and how to adapt

73. Write the text for a video on the best ways to invest small amounts of money

74. Write a bullet-pointed list of the most common financial planning scams and how to avoid them

75. Write a short article on the importance of understanding the role of insurance in a financial plan

76. Write three tweets about the benefits of financial planning for couples and families

77. Write a short blog post on the impact of market conditions on your financial plan and how to adjust accordingly

78. Write the text for a video on the best ways to save for future health care expenses

79. Write a bullet-pointed list of the key considerations for creating a financial plan for a small business

80. Write a short article on the importance of seeking professional financial advice for complex financial planning needs

81. Write three tweets about the importance of saving for retirement in your 20s and 30s

82. Write a short blog post on the basics of investing for beginners

83. Write some ideas for the content of a podcast on the importance of financial planning in everyday life

84. Write a bullet-pointed list of the most common financial planning mistakes and how to avoid them

85. Write a short article on the benefits of having a diversified investment portfolio

86. Write three tweets about the impact of inflation on your financial plan and how to counteract it

87. Write a short blog post on the steps to creating a comprehensive financial plan

88. Write some ideas for the content of a podcast on the benefits of seeking professional financial advice

89. Write a bullet-pointed list of the key considerations for choosing the right

financial adviser

90. Write a short article on the importance of having a long-term investment strategy

91. Write three tweets about the benefits of automating your finances through a financial planning app

92. Write a short blog post on the best ways to reduce monthly expenses in a financial plan

93. Write some ideas for the content of a podcast on the basics of investing in real estate

94. Write a bullet-pointed list of the most common financial planning myths and why they're not true

95. Write a short article on the importance of regularly reviewing and updating your financial plan

96. Write three tweets about the impact of life events on financial planning and how to prepare for them

97. Write a short blog post on the best ways to save for college expenses in a financial plan

98. Write some ideas for the content of a podcast on the basics of insurance and how it relates to financial planning

99. Write a bullet-pointed list of the key elements of a comprehensive financial plan

100. Write a short article on the importance of considering all financial aspects when making big purchases

101. Write three tweets about the benefits of working with a professional financial planner

102. Write a short blog post on the importance of a customised financial plan for achieving financial goals

103. Write the text for a video on the benefits of having a financial planner to provide an unbiased perspective on your finances

104. Write a bullet-pointed list of the advantages of working with a financial planner over managing finances on your own

105. Write a short article on the peace of mind that comes with having a

comprehensive financial plan in place

106. Write three tweets about the benefits of a financial planner's expertise in the financial industry

107. Write a short blog post on the impact of a financial planner's experience and knowledge on your financial plan

108. Write the text for a video on the benefits of having a financial planner as a sounding board for important financial decisions

109. Write a bullet-pointed list of the key services that a financial planner can provide

110. Write a short article on the value of a financial planner's personalised attention and support for your finances

111. Write three tweets about the benefits of having a financial planner as an accountability partner

112. Write a short blog post on the impact of a financial planner's guidance on long-term financial success

113. Write the text for a video on the benefits of having a financial planner to help navigate complex financial decisions

114. Write a bullet-pointed list of the ways a financial planner can help clients reduce financial stress

115. Write a short article on the importance of a financial planner in helping clients create a plan for a secure financial future

116. Write three tweets about the benefits of a financial planner's ability to provide an in-depth analysis of your finances

117. Write a short blog post on the impact of a financial planner's understanding of the latest financial industry trends on your financial plan

118. Write a short blog on how financial planners charge for their services

119. Write the text for a video on the benefits of a financial planner's ability to help clients plan for unexpected events and emergencies

120. Write a bullet-pointed list of the ways a financial planner can help clients make the most of their financial resources

121. Write a short article on the peace of mind that comes with having a trusted financial planner to guide you through life's financial ups and downs

122. Write a branding document for a firm of financial advisers [YOUR BUSINESS NAME] who specialise in [SERVICE] for people who are [AGE and DEMOGRAPHIC] in [LOCATION]

123. Give me some great keywords for a blog about financial planning

124. Create an outline for a blog titled…

125. Turn the transcript for this YouTube video into a blog post

126. Create a promotional email for this blog post

127. Proofread this text

128. Rephrase this blog to be more casual/friendly/serious

129. Generate unique angles or strategies for the topic [your topic]. Emphasise ideas that are fresh and innovative

130. As an Oxford graduate and skilled analyst at a premier market research firm, guide me in crafting marketing content that resonates with [lawyers in London] who are nearing retirement and who are late in starting their financial planning. Emphasise uncommon and expert questions to ask

131. I'm looking for a [type of blog post] that will engage my [ideal client persona] with a unique and compelling perspective on [subject] and encourage them to take [desired action] on my [website/service]

132. I need a [type of blog post] that will provide valuable and relevant information to my [ideal client persona] and encourage them to take [desired action] on my [website/service]

133. I'm looking for a [type of blog post] that will educate my [ideal client persona] on a specific [topic] and encourage them to take [desired action] on my [website/service]

134. I need a [type of blog post] that will speak directly to the needs and pain points of my [ideal client persona] and encourage them to take [desired action] with a sense of urgency and strong offer

135. I'm looking for a [type of blog post] that will showcase the value and benefits of my [service] to [ideal client persona] and convince them to take [desired action] with social proof and credibility-building elements

136. I need a [type of blog post] that will tell a story about my [service] and how it has helped [ideal client persona] achieve their [goal] in a relatable and engaging way

137. I need a [type of blog post] that will tell a story about my [service] and how it has helped [ideal client persona] achieve their [goal] in a relatable and engaging way

138. I'm looking for a [type of blog post] that will draw in my [ideal client persona] with a strong headline and hook, and then convince them to take [desired action] with persuasive professional language and compelling evidence

139. I need a [type of blog post] that will address the pain points and needs of my [ideal client persona] and show them how my [service] is the solution they've been searching for

140. I'm looking for a [type of blog post] that will clearly explain the features and benefits of my [service] to [ideal client persona] and encourage them to engage with me with a strong call-to-action

A few more for good measure:

141. I need a [type of blog post] that will overcome objections and concerns my [ideal client persona] may have about my [service] and convince them to take [desired action]

142. I'm looking for a [type of blog post] that will showcase the unique features and benefits of my [service] to [ideal client persona] and encourage them to engage with me

143. I need a [type of blog post] that will make my [ideal client persona] feel [emotion] about my [service] and encourage them to take [desired action] with a sense of

urgency

144. I'm looking for a [type of blog post] that will establish trust and credibility with my [ideal client persona] by highlighting the successes and testimonials of previous clients who have used my [service]

145. I need a [type of blog post] that will convince my [ideal client persona] to engage with my [service] by highlighting its unique benefits and addressing any potential objections

146. I'm looking for a [type of blog post] that will speak directly to my [ideal client persona] and encourage them to take [desired action] on my [website/service]

For more prompts, join our AI Best Practice Group for Financial Planners at https://ai-best-practice-for-advisers.scoreapp.com

Informing Clients of Your Plans

A Powerful Use of AI

This might seem like a bit of an afterthought, but I have deliberately left this point to the end for good reason, and to show you a specific example of how ChatGPT and the like can be used.

It should go without saying that at some stage in your AI journey you will need to inform clients of your plans. Not only that, but if appropriate, financial advisers should obtain explicit consent from clients regarding the collection, processing and use of their personal data in AI applications.

How you do this and exactly *when* will vary between different firms, so I leave that to you – but clearly you must build it into one of the eight stages highlighted – **or even give it a stage of its own**.

Communicating your plans will be an exciting but delicate stage, requiring skill and tact. But as I've said throughout this book, it's a task that can be helped greatly with the use of Generative AI. But it will take your newfound prompting skills to make it work effectively. So here is an AI prompt that will help and at the very least get you started.

Go to ChatGPT or other Generative AI tool of choice and enter this:

"I want you to imagine that you are the Head of Operations [or whoever is most appropriate within your business] in a financial planning business in the UK.

You are in the process of adopting AI in the business and want to be transparent with clients as to your plans and how AI will be used.

At the same time I don't want to scare clients because some of them may be elderly, vulnerable or concerned about some aspects of the technology. Nevertheless adoption of AI will be of great value ultimately to the financial planning business and its clients.

I want you to create an initial letter that can be sent to clients explaining our plans and briefly highlighting how AI will be used within the business and how it will benefit clients.

The letter needs to be reassuring about data privacy and explain that this is the first such communication, and that as our plans develop over time, further updates will be given in the form of a range of educational materials designed to reassure and answer clients' questions. Nevertheless, clients should be encouraged to get in touch should they have any immediate concerns."

This prompt will 'bake the cake'. You, then add the icing. To take things further you could even ask ChatGPT to write a series of communications for release to clients in various formats over a set period of time. These could include FAQs, slides for a presentation or webinar, informative articles, explanatory pages for your website, scripts for videos, email updates, case studies of how AI will be used in practice – and so on.

You could even ask the AI to write your entire communication plan…

~

There's no denying that the road to adoption of AI in a financial advice business might not always be easy, and on occasion may be bumpy, but with this guide and an AI co-driver at our side to support us, it should be a much smoother ride for everyone.

Glossary of some of the Key Terms related to AI and the Financial Advisory industry.

Decoding the Language of AI

AI (Artificial Intelligence):

The simulation of human intelligence processes by machines, especially computer systems. These processes include learning, reasoning, problem-solving, perception and language understanding.

AI Champion:

An individual within an organisation who promotes and manages the adoption and effective use of AI.

Algorithm:

A step-by-step procedure for solving a problem or accomplishing a task, often employed by AI systems to make decisions or predictions based on input data.

Big Data:

Large volumes of data that can be analysed computationally to reveal patterns, trends and associations, particularly relating to human behaviour and interactions.

Change Management:

The systematic approach to dealing with the transition or transformation of an organisation's goals, processes, or technologies.

Chatbot:

An AI software designed to interact with humans in their natural languages. These interactions can occur through messaging applications, websites, mobile apps or through the telephone.

Data Mining:

The process of discovering patterns and knowledge from large amounts of data. The data sources can include databases, data warehouses, the internet and other information repositories.

Deep Learning:

A subfield of machine learning concerned with algorithms inspired by the structure and function of the brain called artificial neural networks.

GPT (as in ChatGPT):

"GPT" stands for "Generative Pre-training Transformer".

"Generative" means it creates new output (like sentences) from learned patterns.

"Pre-training" means it was initially taught on a vast amount of text data before fine-tuning.

"Transformer" refers to the type of model architecture used, enabling it to understand the context of words in a sentence.

Lifestyle Financial Planning:

A more personalised approach to managing your finances. It involves designing a financial strategy based on your lifestyle, dreams and personal values, not just numeric goals. The focus is on creating a plan that allows you to maintain and enhance your desired lifestyle, both now and in the future.

It encompasses all aspects of financial planning, but the decisions are led by the life you want to lead.

Machine Learning:

A branch of artificial intelligence based on the idea that systems can learn from data, identify patterns and make decisions with minimal human intervention.

Natural Language Processing (NLP):

A branch of artificial intelligence that helps computers understand, interpret and manipulate human language.

Predictive Analytics:

The use of data, statistical algorithms and machine learning techniques to identify the likelihood of future outcomes based on historical data.

Prompt Engineering:

The careful crafting and refinement of instructions or queries given to AI models to elicit desired responses. It is the process of optimising AI models by designing effective prompts to generate accurate and contextually appropriate outputs, enabling more precise and valuable interactions with the AI system.

Robo-advisers:

Digital platforms that provide automated, algorithm-driven financial planning services with little to no human supervision.

Robot Process Automation (RPA):

The use of software with artificial intelligence and machine learning capabilities to handle high-volume, repeatable tasks that previously required humans.

Training Data:

The data used to train an AI or machine learning system. It often consists of input data and the corresponding correct responses.

Newsletter Resource

LifeTalk Insider is the acclaimed weekly Newsletter for Financial Advice Professionals.

Available online or delivered to your inbox, LifeTalk Insider curates the very best content from the main LifeTalk group.

Subscribe at www.lifetalkinsider.com/subscribe

Can I make a request please?

I really hope you have enjoyed this book – please feel free to ask questions at any time by emailing philip@philipcalvert.com.

I would be extremely grateful if you would please consider giving this book a five-star review on Amazon, as this helps us to reach more people – thank you.

About the Author

Philip Calvert is a specialist in helping financial advisers to leverage technology and online professional networking as part of their sales, marketing and communication strategies.

He is in demand as a LinkedIn, technology and social media expert in regulated industries and speaks at conferences and events worldwide. He has presented to over a million financial services delegates around the world.

A small selection of clients Philip has worked with include Standard Life, Scottish Widows, Nucleus, St. James's Place, Schroders Personal Wealth, Openwork, Chase de Vere, Quilter, Key Group, University of Cambridge, Santander, Million Dollar Round Table, Personal Finance Society, Scottish Widows, Maserati, Canon, Fiat, Pfizer, AstraZeneca, Academy for Chief Executives and multiple financial advice firms.

To book Philip to speak at your event or train your adviser team, contact him at philip@philipcalvert.com or through LinkedIn.

Philip's speaking and training topics for financial advisers include:

- How to attract more of your ideal clients and connections with LinkedIn

- Successful marketing and lead generation for financial advisers

- How to use scorecard marketing to attract higher quality, higher converting leads

- How to plan, promote and present successful seminars, workshops and client events

- How to plan, promote and present successful webinars and online client events

- Professional presentation and public speaking skills for financial advisers

- Fifty new income streams for financial advisers

- How to write your first book

- How to use AI for Marketing and Communications

Other Books for Financial Advisers by Philip Calvert

Marketing and Lead Generation for Financial Advice Professionals: From Prospects to Profits – Proven Strategies for Financial Advisers to Attract More of their Ideal Clients

LinkedIn Lead Generation for Financial Advisers: How to Attract More of Your Ideal Clients on LinkedIn – Proven Messaging Scripts and Daily Planner

Successful Seminar Selling for Financial Advisers: The Financial Planner's Guide to Attracting Profitable New Leads through Seminars, Workshops & Client Events

56 New Income Streams for Financial Advisers: How to Turn your Financial Planning Expertise & Experience into Profitable Information Products for the Digital Age

amazon

Disclaimer and Terms of Use

This book is provided for educational and informational purposes specifically tailored to financial advisers exploring AI adoption. Resale or distribution rights of any portion of this publication are strictly prohibited. Only authorised purchasers are permitted to access its contents. Unauthorised transmission or reproduction of this material in any form without prior written consent from the author is prohibited and subject to legal action for copyright infringement.

The information, services and resources presented in this book are based on the current AI landscape in the financial advising industry. While the techniques discussed offer significant potential and success for financial advisers globally, it's important to acknowledge that the internet is dynamic and certain websites or services mentioned may undergo changes, cessation or expansion over time.

We strive to equip readers with adaptable skills and knowledge to navigate the evolving internet and marketing environment. However, we cannot be held responsible for changes that may affect the applicability or effectiveness of the techniques presented herein.

Any earnings, income statements, or results mentioned are estimates based on our own experiences and those of other marketers. They are provided as examples and do not guarantee individual success. Numerous factors, including work ethic and market conditions, can influence personal outcomes. Readers must assume the entire risk and responsibility for any decision to rely on the figures provided.

Product names, logos and artwork mentioned in this book are copyrights of their respective owners. Their inclusion does not imply sponsorship or endorsement of this publication.

While efforts have been made to ensure the accuracy of the information provided, the author assumes no responsibility for errors, omissions, or misinterpretations. Any perceived slights towards individuals or organisations are unintentional. Readers are responsible for their use of the materials and information contained herein.

No guarantees of income or specific results are made. The author reserves the right to make changes and accepts no liability on behalf of any purchaser or reader of this material.

From time to time, the author may include hyperlinks to external products and services, some of which may be affiliate links. The author may receive a commission if readers make a purchase through these links.

Readers assume full responsibility for compliance and compliant use of the material presented in this book, as defined by their respective regulatory bodies. The author makes no guarantees that the ideas presented will align with the local compliance regime of individual readers.

Your Notes

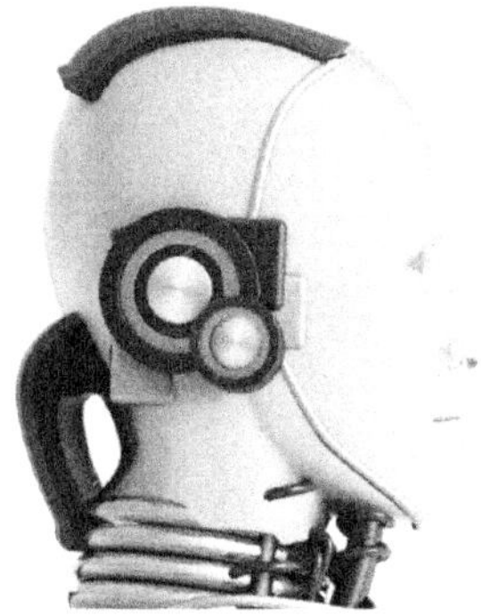

Printed in Great Britain
by Amazon

24210249R00136